ENDORSEMENTS

The prophetic ministry is intriguing to all and a mystery to most. Perhaps because we are drawn to its uniqueness and those who operate in this dimension. Also, because most who operate in the prophetic are not able to demystify it by definition or include us in their journey. Prophet Rob Sanchez has done us a favor and a great service by allowing us into his life and journey with accuracy and precision. All who read *Discovering and Releasing Your Prophetic Voice* will see, hear, and function more clearly.

—Bishop Michael Pitts
Cornerstone Global Network
www.michaelpitts.com

Discovering and Releasing Your Prophetic Voice encapsulates a level of revelational insight that can only be acquired by one who has walked, stumbled, and run with the prophetic mantle. Prophet Rob has allowed the various seasons that come with such a lifestyle to sharpen the wisdom and knowledge produced from such a mantle. I highly recommend *Discovering and Releasing Your Prophetic Voice* to anyone with a desire to embark on their own prophetic journey as God develops and sharpens the gift within them.

—Prophet Ruckins McKinley, D.D.
Senior Pastor, New Breed Worship Center

The prophetic ministry is one shrouded with intrigue and mystery. Rob Sanchez has the unique ability to unlock the mystery of prophetic ministry through practical application. It takes a special prophetic mantle to help others see prophetic potential and learn how to unlock it. Rob is uniquely called and gifted to do just that. *Discovering and Releasing Your Prophetic Voice* is something I would recommend to everyone.

—Joey Zamora
Senior Pastor, Cornerstone Church Tri-Cities

Prophet Rob Sanchez is a dear friend of mine who has given me an incalculable number of prophetic words that have all been very good and encouraging to my life. Jeremiah 1:5 says, "Before I formed you in the womb I knew you… I ordained you a prophet to the nations." I believe this verse describes Rob; he is a prophetic voice who is making an impact. This book, *Discovering and Releasing Your Prophetic Voice*, will provide limitless blessings for those who read it. He brings heaven to earth and encourages us to shift our mindset and have a heavenly perspective.

—Dr. Keith Ellis, Th.D.
Author of *One Minute With God: Sixty Supernatural Seconds that will Change Your Life*

Monday, Sept. 13, 2021
rec'd from Sid Roth (35. 15.)
• This Bk
• 3 CD's } Prophecy

DISCOVERING & RELEASING YOUR

PROPHETIC VOICE

DISCOVERING & RELEASING YOUR PROPHETIC VOICE

HOW EVERYDAY PEOPLE CAN OPERATE IN THE PROPHETIC DIMENSION

ROB SANCHEZ

DESTINY IMAGE® PUBLISHERS, INC.
P.O. Box 310, Shippensburg, PA 17257-0310
"Promoting Inspired Lives."

This book and all other Destiny Image and Destiny Image Fiction books are available at Christian bookstores and distributors worldwide.

Cover design by Eileen Rockwell
Interior design by Susan Ramundo

For more information on foreign distributors, call 717-532-3040.
Reach us on the Internet: www.destinyimage.com.

ISBN 13 TP: 978-0-7684-5750-6
ISBN 13 eBook: 978-0-7684-5751-3
ISBN 13 HC: 978-0-7684-5753-7
ISBN 13 LP: 978-0-7684-5752-0

For Worldwide Distribution, Printed in the U.S.A.
1 2 3 4 5 6 7 8 / 25 24 23 22 21

CONTENTS

FOREWORD

The prophet is a spiritual leader, one who declares the oracles of God. Indeed, the prophet is a gift to the Church.

> *Now these are the gifts Christ gave to the church: the apostles, the prophets, the evangelists, and the pastors and teachers. Their responsibility is to equip God's people to do his work and build up the church, the body of Christ* (Ephesians 4:11-12, NLT).

The Scripture clearly teaches that the office of the prophet, along with the other leadership offices, comes with a heavy weight of responsibility, a mandate to properly equip God's people. To be a prophet of God is a divine calling, a heavenly assignment.

In addition to the prophetic office, God has also graced His Church with believers who operate in prophetic gifts.

> *He gives one person the power to perform miracles, and another the ability to prophesy* (1 Corinthians 12:10, NLT).

Together, both the operation and the office of the prophetic work to guide, lead, encourage, comfort, and edify God's people.

But he that prophesieth speaketh unto men to edification, and exhortation, and comfort (1 Corinthians 14:3, KJV).

Whether you're called to carry the influence and leadership authority that come with the office of the prophet or you desire to operate in a prophetic gift, you desire a good thing. And the very fact that you are reading this book on the prophetic is an indicator that you have a spiritual hunger for the glorious working that is prophetic ministry.

Now, among all of the five office gifts mentioned in the book of Ephesians, perhaps the most often criticized and most intensely scrutinized is the office of the prophet.

Certainly, in the world of the prophetic, there have been abuses. There have been issues. There have been fakes. And there have been those who were prematurely released into ministry. Social media can provide a platform to anyone who wants it, whether or not they have gone through the spiritual process of maturing. Anyone can claim a title. Anyone can skip the process. Anyone can claim to be prophetic.

Many apply psychology and call it discernment. Some practice cold reading and call it the word of knowledge. And others make guesses about the future and call it prophecy. Life coaching and commercialization have polluted the prophetic. No doubt, there are frauds who flood our social media time lines, televisions, and pulpits. They prophesy from their imaginations.

> *Then this message came to me from the LORD: "Son of man, prophesy against the false prophets of Israel who are inventing their own prophecies. Say to them, 'Listen to the word of the LORD. This is what the Sovereign LORD says: What sorrow awaits the false prophets who are following their own imaginations and have seen nothing at all!'"* (Ezekiel 13:1-3, NLT)

Yet, I'm encouraged. The existence of a counterfeit implies the existence of the genuine.

While many have emphasized prophetic "accuracy," I can hear the Holy Spirit calling our attention to prophetic purity. When a true prophetic gift is operating, there's no need for gimmicks, techniques, or tricks. A prophet either hears from God or keeps quiet. True prophets are always more concerned with what God is actually saying than they are with what people want to hear. They get their messaging straight from heaven. They say what God says. Period. We need more true prophets—people who will communicate the heart of God, shun the evils of prophecy-for-pay, and spend hours locked away with the Holy Spirit.

This is why I'm so thankful to the Lord for the prophetic ministry of my friend, Robert Sanchez. I've known Prophet Rob for over 15 years. I've had the joy of hosting Prophet Rob on my program, ministering alongside of him in conferences, and fellowshipping with him as a brother. I've shared meals with him. Our families know each other. Our ministry teams help each other. And I truly believe that Prophet Rob is the real deal. He loves the Lord, loves people, and cares deeply for his friends and family. I appreciate his strong gift, and I honor his character.

Throughout my years of friendship with Prophet Rob, I've been thrilled to witness his gift in operation. More times than I can count, I've thrown up my hands and exclaimed, "Only God could reveal this!" I've watched Prophet Rob prophesy in churches, conferences, restaurants, and everyday settings.

And Prophet Rob doesn't just prophesy powerfully, he studies God's Word diligently. In almost every conversation, Prophet Rob enthusiastically shares with me his latest biblical study. He's a man who loves the Word and loves the prophetic. He's highly gifted in both. Those two areas of gifting are on full display in this book.

In *Discovering and Releasing Your Prophetic Voice*, Prophet Rob shares his many insights that he has gleaned over decades of proven and tested prophetic ministry. He strategically threads together stories from his life with biblical revelations about the prophetic. I know that you'll be both inspired and informed as you read through this great work.

If you believe that God has called you to the prophetic, you should pay close attention to the writings found within these pages. You're getting decades of lessons in one book. Learn from it. Apply it. And let the truths within activate and accelerate your prophetic gifting.

May the Holy Spirit bring impartation as you read.

—David Diga Hernandez
Evangelist and Friend of the Holy Spirit
www.DavidHernandezMinistries.com

INTRODUCTION

The prophetic lifestyle is a lifestyle of consecration, obedience, faith, and intimacy with God. I am a prophet, and I want to see the awakening of the prophetic within you.

Since the days of old and up until this very moment, prophets have been speaking. The prophetic is active and alive in the earth today, and if you are reading this it is because you are drawn to the prophetic. Your heart seeks after the deeper things of God. If you are drawn to the prophetic, it is likely because you are a prophetic person. I know that it is divine destiny that is causing your eyes to fall upon these words. I believe that there is a prophetic spirit within you. If you dare to believe it, you very well may be counted among God's prophetic people, established and destined by His sovereign will.

Prophetic people are peculiar and powerful, unique and insightful. We are gifted to operate in ways that make the skeptics believers and the believers doers. We do not always quite fit in, yet we can be found most often where God needs us to be—meeting divine appointments.

As one of God's anointed oracles, I, as a prophet, speak words of hope and life. I declare light in dark places, speak freedom over the oppressed, and sometimes witness the future before it unfolds. Prophets are the keepers of the secrets of God and the stewards of His mysteries. Where others see defeat, I see destiny. What others overlook, I understand. The prophetic anointing is "in your face," strange, and at times uncomfortable. At the same time, I am God's statement piece, His purposeful art, and an expression of His heart.

Now you may be asking, "But Prophet Rob, how do I really know you are talking about me? How do I know if I am actually called to the prophetic?"

> *Let love be your highest goal! But you should also desire the special abilities the Spirit gives—especially the ability to prophesy* (1 Corinthians 14:1).

Every Spirit-filled follower of Jesus can prophesy and walks in some level of the prophetic, whether they realize it or not. Prophecy can be as simple as giving a word of encouragement in the form of a Bible verse. The prophetic doesn't have to be complicated, and it shouldn't be spooky.

> *But one who prophesies strengthens others, encourages them, and comforts them. A person who speaks in tongues is strengthened personally, but one who speaks a word of prophecy strengthens the entire church* (1 Corinthians 14:3-4).

Whether you are drawn to the prophetic, or whether you know that you are a prophet because you have been called into that office, *Discovering and Releasing Your Prophetic Voice* is going to be an invigorating, faith-inspiring read for you. I pray that you soon learn to yield your life into the hand of God and what He wants to share through you. It's time to add your voice to the sound coming from heaven that is speaking God's message of love for mankind.

Throughout my years of prophetic ministry, I have learned many lessons and witnessed countless miracles. The Lord has taught me, through pain and process, keys to developing and operating in the prophetic. And now, I want to share those keys with you.

I believe everyone is able to flow in the prophetic in some way, shape, or form. If you sense that pull into the prophetic ministry, then follow it through. Connect and sit under a prophetic ministry in order for you to learn and grow. When you submit yourself to someone (such as a pastor, church leader, spiritual father/mother) whom you can glean from, a deepening of the gifts will come. Growth comes through relationship, submission, and accountability.

I believe that destiny has brought you to this very moment. So allow me to share with you my journey. I pray that you absorb the truths that unfold as you read through the pages of this book. This book is a big piece of my prophetic story during my journey so far. In the time that it takes you to read this book, you will have received insight, wisdom, and revelation from over 20 years of prophetic ministry. I know this will accelerate your growth. Through stories and scriptures, I am imparting to you a portion of my experience and the growth that has taken place in my life. As you learn more about the prophetic, the prophetic will be stirred in you. It's time to ignite the prophetic sound within you.

CHAPTER 1

SET APART

CLIMBING MOUNT MURUD

In 2001, I, along with several pastors, accepted an invitation to preach in Malaysia for 18 days at the Mt. Murud Prayer Mountain of All Nations. The invitation came months before the actual event. The host ministry wanted to give us ample time to prepare—to prepare for the ministry, to prepare travel arrangements, and to prepare for the daunting climb.

Yes, a climb. As in, I was going to literally climb a mountain.

The prayer center was located at the very top of the mountain. The climb from base camp, we were told, was a challenging one. We were highly encouraged to train and condition to make the climb. At the time, I was very heavy; I weighed somewhere between 250 and 260 pounds. I can tell you that I was most certainly not in an ideal shape to make an 8,000-foot climb through some jungle on a mountain.

Though I looked forward to ministering, I did not look forward to the climb. Imagine having to trek up a mountain and then passionately preach a prayer conference after the climb. And not only would I be preaching, I would be prophesying. And when I prophesy, I do not just minister to one or two; I spend hours speaking over as many as possible. I truly pour myself out mentally, physically, spiritually into times of prophetic ministry.

Still several weeks away, I received a phone call from the gentleman who was planning the trip. I was completely relieved when he told me that because I was one of the conference speakers, a helicopter would be taking me to the top of the mountain. The idea of preparing physically for the climb was thrown out of my mind. And I was glad. *Thank You, Jesus,* I thought to myself.

The trip date came and I arrived at the base of the 8,000-foot mountain. There, a couple of pastors and leaders gathered at base camp for tea and fellowship. We were to spend the night at the camp, and those making the climb would do it first thing in the morning. I enjoyed the sights, sounds, and tastes of the mission field while having some wonderful conversations with men of faith.

After the fellowship, everyone settled into their own sleeping quarters to rest for the night. Expectation filled our hearts as we looked forward to the next day—a day of ministry, a day of Kingdom expansion, a day of helicopter rides instead of mountain climbs. I recall sitting across the table from a well-respected Malaysian pastor and happily saying, "Good night. I'll see you on the helicopter tomorrow."

That night, as I slept, the Lord visited me in a dream. His instructions were simple, "I want you to climb the mountain, for it will be a great testimony. Rob, I want you to climb it to the top like Moses."

When I woke up the next morning, the first thing I thought was, *Lord, do I really have to hike up this mountain?* I much preferred the helicopter, but the Lord was faithful to give me confirmation. Just about an hour or so after I woke up, a friend of mine approached me and said, "Rob, I really feel strongly that, like Moses, we're supposed to climb to the top of this mountain." I told him, "The Lord spoke the same thing to me last night in a dream." I accepted the climb as a mandate from the Lord. I didn't know why He wanted me to climb it, nor did I know what would come of me climbing it. I just knew that the Lord wanted me to do it. So I determined to obey the voice of God.

I was accompanied by Malaysian guides who informed me that it was in my best interests to not make the climb in my jeans. So we stopped by a shop where I bought the largest pair of shorts I could find. But being a 250-pound man in an Asian nation, I had no success in finding shorts that were my size. What I did find was a pair of shorts that they told me were a size 4XL. That's what they told me, but trust me when I tell you that the sizing standards are much different in Malaysia than in America.

Also, the weather was cold and rainy, so I was given a poncho to help me stay dry. So there I was, a large man in little shorts and a poncho.

I remember smiling and telling the Lord, "You really do have a sense of humor." I can only imagine what I must have looked like from His perspective, and I am sure He enjoyed a fun laugh.

The journey began.

We followed the path up the mountain, but it was not a clear path by any means. It was not a paved or dirt road, nor were there any steps anywhere to aid our ascension. The clearing we walked through was scarcely there and it was obstructed by twigs, plants, and rocks. The entire way up the mountain, I was slipping and falling. My legs got scratched by protruding branches and sticks. I was muddy, cold, wet, and tired.

Occasionally, I could hear a helicopter pass over my head. I would look up with longing, wishing I was on one of those helicopters. Each time one would pass, I would think, *Man, I should have been on that helicopter.* Instead of flying through the air, I was trudging through the mud.

I pressed forward.

After a couple of hours of shoving aside wild plants and grabbing ahold of barely stable branches for balance, we came to a bridge that definitely wasn't designed for a man like me. It was a narrow bridge, about 24 inches wide. As I squeezed onto it and moved across the old ropes and wood, I slipped and fell on the rain-soaked bridge.

My shin smashed onto one of the wooden steps and began to swell. I was bruised and bloodied, exhausted and frustrated. I cried out, "Why am I climbing this mountain? I don't understand. I'm not fit for this. And there are perfectly good helicopters rushing over my head." Just after saying that, I fell again, and when I did I reached for what I thought was a rail—it was a loose branch. In the fall, I injured my back.

But I got up and continued to climb.

Finally, and to my much-desired relief, I reached the top of the mountain and was taken to my quarters to get a little rest before ministering that evening. My sleeping quarters weren't much. It was a small, rundown cabin with a hardwood floor, a tiny fiery stove that made the room glow orange with warmth, and a little mat on the floor in the corner of my room. But to me in that moment, that little mat was a king-sized luxury mattress.

It never felt so good to fall onto the floor. That tiny mat was my escape. Within seconds of plopping onto my luxury mat, I fell asleep. I don't know how long I was asleep before I was awakened by one of my hiking guides.

Knocking on my door, the messenger startled me from sleep. With his head down and his shoulders forward, he softly and slowly stepped into my room. When he looked up at me, I saw sorrow in his eyes. His lips quivered as he said, "Please, come. There's been a tragedy." In my spirit, I already knew what had happened.

The fifth helicopter—the one I was scheduled to be on—crashed. Everyone on board perished. The Malaysian pastor with whom I enjoyed tea the evening before and to whom I said, "I'll see you on the helicopter," was among those killed in the crash.

Then, all of it made sense—the exhaustion, the journey, the injuries, all of it.

It was then that I knew why the Lord had spoken to me in a dream. His voice spared my life. At the time, my wife, Juanita, was home because she was pregnant with my first daughter, Zoe. My daughter hadn't even moved in the womb yet. What would they have done if I was killed in the helicopter crash?

What would have happened had I not obeyed the Lord? What will happen if you do not obey the voice of God in your life?

There is a call upon your life. You've been set apart for a Kingdom purpose. When God sets you apart, He guides you in the path of His protection.

I know this to be true. In fact, God has been protecting me since the day I was born.

MY BIRTH

I am a twin. My sister, delivered naturally at birth, was born 99 minutes before I was. My sister was born on the second floor of the hospital. I was born on the third. Normally, doctors like to see twins born within 15 minutes of each other, but this birth was a bit different. Though my twin sister was born naturally, I made my way into the world via C-section. My mother delivered my sister with no complications. However, there was trouble with me. Complications had made it so my mother and I were both at risk. Simply put, I was positioned sideways in the womb, so if my mother had continued pushing with the contractions, there was a high probability that my neck would break during a natural delivery.

Not wanting to risk my life, the doctor informed my mother of the plan to proceed with a C-section. There was only one problem: The anesthesiologist was stuck in traffic on his way to the hospital and wouldn't arrive for about an hour. The doctor rolled up a towel and put it in my mother's mouth. He instructed, "Every time you feel a contraction, do not push; bite down. Biting down will weaken the force of the contractions." So, as instructed, every time my mother had a contraction, she would bite down. While my mother fought the natural physical reactions to being in labor, the doctor stepped outside of the delivery room and into the hallway to speak privately with my father. It was then that my father was presented with a very difficult choice. The doctor asked, "If we can only save one of them, who do you want us to save, your wife or your son?" Stunned by the question, my father asked, "What will I do with seven kids and no wife?" The urgency of the matter did not afford my father a pause to contemplate. He decided, "If you have to save one, save my wife; but do everything you can to save both. I want both."

Without making a promise, the doctor offered only "to do his best," attempting to save two precious lives.

At that point in his life, my father knew only one prayer—the Lord's Prayer. Helpless and unable to do anything in the natural, my father did all that he was able to do in the spiritual. He dropped to his knees and prayed that simple prayer, again and again.

Back in the delivery room, my mother was becoming delirious. In the midst of the chaos, dazed by a weakened state of mind and body, my mother fixed her thoughts on the Lord. Exhausted and desperate, she cried out, "Lord, if You save my son, I'll dedicate him to You all the days of his life." My mother recalls feeling the hand of an angel touch her the moment she prayed that prayer—it very well could have been the hand of the Lord, because by that touch, she was filled with peace.

Critical minutes passed, a total of 99—and then a miracle happened. The anesthesiologist finally arrived and my mother was taken to the third floor of the hospital to have the C-section.

I was born a healthy baby boy. Along with my mother, I had survived. I was so healthy that I was actually released from the hospital a day before my sister.

In the same way that I have been preserved, so God also preserves you. But being set apart is more than divine protection on its own. As children of God, you've been set apart, marked as a unique instrument in the intentional hand of God. If you think back with enough focus, I know you'll recall some form of heavenly contact, some special moment when God touched your life. I can recall such a moment.

BAPTIZED IN THE HOLY SPIRIT

My dad was a part of a music ministry team that would perform at juvenile halls, prisons, and senior homes. He also ministered in churches. Before ministering, my dad and the members of his music team would meet early in the morning to pray and practice their worship music. Often, they would have their pre-ministry prayer meetings in our home.

One Saturday morning, when I was about nine years old, I was awakened by the sound of people passionately praying. There were over a dozen of them praying in my living room. Thirsty, I got out of bed and made my way toward the kitchen. The group, praying in tongues and worshiping aloud with fervency, had formed a circle and was blocking my way to the refrigerator. And because their hands were joined, I struggled to break through the group. So I decided to duck under their hands as I moved through the living room and into the kitchen.

I managed to make it to the refrigerator to get myself a drink of milk. After I enjoyed my refreshing drink, I put my glass on the counter and made my way out of the kitchen in the same manner I entered—through the prayer circle and under joined hands. But this time, when I went through the prayer circle, something peculiar happened.

I walked in to get a drink, but I left with something more. Without coercion or suggestion, without anyone laying hands on me, I received a gift. On my way out of the kitchen and through the prayer circle, I began to pray in tongues. The gift just began to flow naturally. I was filled with the Holy Spirit.

Unaware of my newly received spiritual gift, my mother pulled me aside and sternly warned, "Son, you can't walk under the prayer circle like that. It's irreverent." I was so excited about the gift I had received that I did not even think to reply to her point. "Mom!" I shouted, "I can do what you and Dad can do!" Curious, she asked, "What do you mean that you can do what Dad and I can do?" I gladly announced, "I can pray like you!" And then I began to pray in tongues right in front of her.

To my surprise, my mother did not respond with elation; she responded with worry. "Son, do not do that. You are blaspheming the Holy Spirit." The puzzled look on my face nudged her to explain, "You see, your Dad and I are filled with the Holy Spirit, so we are praying in tongues. You are just making noise."

I must explain to you that my mother was well intentioned. She did not mean to stifle me or the Holy Spirit. She was genuinely concerned that I was just making the noises—or mimicking the gift. My parents did not understand what we now understand: I received the baptism of the Holy Spirit when I walked through that prayer circle.

I know I received the baptism of the Holy Spirit that day because of the way I was guided by the Holy Spirit from then on. My testimony is the evidence.

Often, you'll hear stories about ex-satanists, ex-drug addicts, ex-criminals, and so forth. But my testimony isn't as flashy, and it definitely doesn't seem as interesting as those extreme testimonies. You see, my testimony isn't about what God delivered me from; the power of my testimony is in what He kept me from.

God kept me walking in purity. I never touched drugs or alcohol. I did not hang with the wrong crowd or get into trouble. God spared me from that. He kept me on the right track. He guided me along the path of purity. From the very moment I walked through that prayer circle, I have felt the hand of God on my life. It's simple, really, but powerful all the same. So don't think you need a radical testimony in order to do something for the Kingdom of God; also, don't think your past disqualifies you. As long as you are willing to be used, God will flow through you.

YOU ARE SET APART

When considering the manner in which the Lord will set apart an individual for a specific call or purpose, I think of Samuel the prophet.

> *Samuel did not yet know the Lord because he had never had a message from the Lord before. So the Lord called a third time, and once more Samuel got up and went to Eli. "Here I am. Did you call me?"*
>
> *Then Eli realized it was the Lord who was calling the boy. So he said to Samuel, "Go and lie down again, and if someone calls again, say, 'Speak, Lord, your servant is listening.'" So Samuel went back to bed.*
>
> *And the Lord came and called as before, "Samuel! Samuel!"*
>
> *And Samuel replied, "Speak, your servant is listening"* (1 Samuel 3:7-10).

Samuel the prophet was marked at a young age. Even though he did not at first recognize the voice of God, Samuel was a prophet nonetheless. So do not be discouraged if you have not yet recognized the unique mark of God upon your life.

When I received my first prophetic word, I didn't realize that's what it was. I wasn't even saved at the time. It was the spring of 1993 and I was in my Oral Communications class at the Academy of Arts in San Francisco, California. I had just finished presenting (and failing) a speech when my professor, Robert Ponte, addressed me in front of the entire class. Once I sat down, he looked at me and said, "You, Mr. Robert Sanchez, are by far one of the most gifted speakers in this class." I looked at him wondering if he had listened to the speech I just gave because if he had been paying attention to it, he would not have said that statement. Mr. Ponte continued, "Matter of fact, at ten years into your photography career, you will come to a crossroads in your life. You will put down your camera and never pick it up again. You will become what you're meant to be, an oracle. You will travel all over the world to speak, and many will come to hear you because you will bring a message of hope."

When he finished talking to me, I started thinking about what he said. Not about being an oracle, not about people hearing my message of hope; I thought about what was going to happen at the ten-year mark of my photography career. He said I was going to put down my camera and never pick it up again. *What?!*

Photography was all I knew. It was all I wanted. I was planning to travel and shoot for fashion magazines. I wanted to make a name for myself in the photography world. I never imagined that word would actually come to pass, because photography was my life. What Mr. Ponte said had even angered me, but it also made me wonder. But just like Samuel, I didn't recognize this as the voice of God. Mr. Ponte never said, "Thus says the Lord," or "I hear the Lord saying," yet it didn't change the fact that God wanted to get my attention and used my Oral Communications teacher to plant the seed.

At that moment, I had already invested eight years of my life in studying and crafting my photography business. There was no way I was giving up my dream, so I continued with my life as if nothing had happened. A couple of weeks later it was the day before Easter. My sister Ernestine called me and asked, "Precious, would you do me a favor?" Now, you have to understand something. Whenever Ernestine called me "Precious," it was because she wanted me to do something for her—wash her car, get her food, things like that. So, of course, I felt bad telling her no. I asked her what favor she wanted. "Will you go to church with me tomorrow?" Considering I was a CEO Christian (Christmas, Easter Only), I figured I was fulfilling my obligation and at the same time I wouldn't hurt her feelings, so I told her "Yes." What I didn't know was that she had been praying for me to get saved.

I met Ernestine the next morning at the Baptist church she was attending. We walked in and found a seat toward the back of the church in a row where no one else was sitting. From the moment we walked in, I felt uncomfortable. After being there a couple of minutes, Ernestine said to me, "I'll be right back. I'm going to say 'hi' to some people." She left and didn't come back. I was left sitting all alone. I was thinking about leaving, but then the service started. The choir came up, and as they began to sing I felt something strange inside of me. I felt like crying and I didn't know why. The feeling so overwhelmed me that I thought to myself, *I need to get out of here*. As I tried to stand, I literally felt a presence push me back down into my seat and hold me there. Tears flowed out of my eyes and I couldn't stop them. I don't remember what song the choir sang or the sermon the minister spoke. All I remember is the rush of love that came over me. I said silently, "God, if You're real, come into my life." From that day on, my life was transformed. No one had to invite me to church anymore. No one had to wake me up on Sunday morning. I just went.

I hadn't been looking for God, but He was obviously looking for me. First Samuel 3:7 was definitely a verse that described me. I didn't know the Lord because I had never had a message from Him, or so I thought. God had been trying to get my attention but I never realized it. He set me apart for His purpose and placed a unique mark on my life, just as He did with Samuel.

Don't worry, I didn't forget about the word Robert Ponte gave me about the crossroads I would come to at ten years into my photography career. You'll just have to wait until later in this book to read the rest of that story. (Hint: The story is in Chapter 2.)

Everyone is set apart to do something for God's purpose, but we need to be willing to search out what that purpose is for our life. The very fact that you are reading this journal of my prophetic experiences is proof that something within you is drawn to the prophetic. It is in you, a part of your spiritual DNA.

You might as well just embrace the reality now—you are set apart for this.

Notes on Your Prophetic Journey

Notes on Your Prophetic Journey

CHAPTER 2

RADICAL OBEDIENCE

THROWING DOWN THE PULPIT

During a three-day revival in the city of Seattle, I witnessed a powerful move of the prophetic anointing. During that revival, people received salvation, healing, and prophetic revelation from Heaven. But the revival did not begin with an ease in spiritual flow. It began with some demonic resistance. God tends to send His prophets to the spiritually dull places. Prophets are God's vessels for restoring color and life and for destroying stubborn spiritual obstructions.

It was day number one of the prophetic meetings. For that entire day, before I had even stepped foot into the church building, I had visions of myself ministering. The Lord kept showing me a vision of myself throwing the podium onto the ground. I couldn't get that image out of my head. The Lord was speaking to me about it all day. As odd as it seems, I tell you that the Lord wanted me to throw that church's podium on the ground.

So on the first night of the revival, before any of the miracles started flowing and before the prophetic was freely operational, while I was standing in the worship service, I heard the Lord speak. He said, "Rob, this church is stuck under the steeple of religion. The people need to be freed. I brought you here to shake the people from complacency and move them into a place of spiritual revival and awakening. They are stagnant."

So there I was, ministering on that first night of revival, and the Lord spoke, "Rob, throw down their pulpit." Because I was young, not only in age but also in ministry, I debated within my heart. I thought, *But that would be disrespectful. What will they think of me? I can't do that. What if it's just me?* I reasoned myself out of a response, and I simply refused to do it.

The service was nothing like what I was used to—there was just such a spiritual stagnation in the atmosphere. I preached the rest of my message, gave a few prophetic words, and went home.

When I got home, I felt a deep, heavy sorrow. I felt shattered within. It was an ugly feeling. I knew it was the sorrow of the Spirit that troubled me. I had broken His heart. I heard the voice of the Lord say, "You are *My* prophet. You have been called by *My* name. Trust in Me, and I will not fail you. Like Jeremiah, I've given you a face like flint. You do not have to worry about the faces or the actions of others, for I am in control."

I wept and repented before God. "Lord," I cried, "if this is really You, sometime later, give me another opportunity and I will obey You." The Lord is truly merciful; He gave me another chance.

Saturday night, the church was packed. God was moving, and I was prophesying. I sensed the stirring of the Spirit deep within my soul. Like fire, a holy zeal arose in me. In that moment, God spoke again, "Throw down their pulpit." That time, without hesitation, I took their pulpit and threw it to the ground. A gasp from the crowd filled the air, as the top of the podium broke off as soon as it hit the floor. The podium was broken into two pieces.

No longer worried about the opinion of man, I then took a pitcher of water and began to pour water over the pulpit. I prophesied, "That which has been dead will now come to life. The places where God's presence has been removed will be filled again. I sprinkle water—it's a sign that there is a refreshing and a revival now coming."

Some people became furious. Their faces made that obvious to me. A hush dominated the room.

Just then, one of the oldest members of the church—he was a member of that church for generations—stood up and said, "Everything that this man has said is of God. When I saw him throw down the pulpit, I wanted to tackle him, but the Lord said, 'Look!' And out of the pulpit, I saw demons and unclean spirits fleeing. They came out of the pulpit and fled from the building."

Revival was sparked. The meetings were set ablaze with a holy fire, and that church was taken out of stagnation. Thankfully, the pulpit was later repaired—you couldn't even tell there was ever a fracture. But God used the prophetic action to break the power of a religious spirit.

Sometimes God will ask you to do something radical. When moving in the prophetic gift, you cannot allow the opinion of man to hinder your obedience toward God. At times what you say will be in the face of others and their stuff and won't make sense. Sometimes it will shock or even anger people. You have to be ready and prepared for what God asks you to do. But when you do it in His love, the words that you say will be like a hammer set against stony hearts, breaking down walls and allowing God to enter.

But radical obedience doesn't stop at overcoming the fear of man. Radical obedience will require that you overcome fear, period. Sometimes what God asks you to do will challenge you. But you have been called by *His* name. Your only concern should be whether or not you have obeyed what God has told you to do. Nothing should stop you from obeying God's voice.

Being afraid is normal; everyone feels fear when God challenges them to do something. But the important thing is not allowing that fear to limit you or hold you back. Even Jeremiah was fearful when God called him as a prophet.

> *Then said I: "Ah, Lord God! Behold, I cannot speak, for I am a youth."*
>
> *But the Lord said to me: "Do not say, 'I am a youth,' for you shall go to all to whom I send you, and whatever I command you, you shall speak. Do not be afraid of their faces, for I am with you to deliver you," says the Lord.*
>
> *Then the Lord put forth His hand and touched my mouth, and the Lord said to me: "Behold, I have put My words in your mouth. See, I have this day set you over the nations and over the kingdoms, to root out and to pull down, to destroy and to throw down, to build and to plant"* (Jeremiah 1:6-10 NKJV).

God assured Jeremiah of His presence and the purpose in his life. You can also be secure that God will not leave your side as you walk out His purpose for your life. You are an overcomer.

THE EAGLE'S NEST OFFERING

In 1995, when I was 24 years old, I was a part of a ministry team called Imeon. On one occasion, we traveled as a group from northern California all the way down to southern California to attend a prophetic meeting and hear a man preach named Pastor

Gary Greenwald. At first, I wasn't going to go, but something in my spirit told me that I absolutely had to go to that meeting. So it was at the last minute that I decided to get my plane ticket and join the group.

With me on the trip, I brought along my passion. By that, I mean that I brought my professional photography equipment, including my Canon camera. At the time, it was top of the line. As you read in the previous chapter, I loved doing photography, not just as a hobby, but it was also my way of earning a living. I figured I could take pictures of the prophetic meeting for the sake of memories.

During the service, Pastor Gary ministered a word called, "Lay Down Your Isaac." It was a message about sacrifice, passing divine tests, and how God returned Isaac to Abraham. As an illustration for the message, Pastor Gary challenged everyone in attendance to give something of value in the offering. Pastor Gary wasn't shy about it either. "Whatever you value; it doesn't have to be just money. Give whatever God tells you to give. Lay it down like Abraham laid down Isaac." He explained that he would then give away the items in the offering to others in attendance. He determined who would receive the items from the offering by a game of Bible Trivia. It was a different way of doing things, for sure. There I was with my camera strapped to my neck, because I did not want to miss the perfect shot during the meeting. I would soon wish that I had left the camera in northern California.

We're going to pause for a second here because if you are like me, once you read the words, "Lay Down Your Isaac," you probably flipped back to the story in Chapter 1 where I received the prophetic word from my college professor. Remember, I received that word in the spring of 1993, eight years into my photography career. Now it's September 1995, two years later. Yes, the crossroads is here.

Alright, now back to the story...

During the offering, the Spirit of the Lord asked me a most challenging question, "Rob, do you love Me?" Without hesitation, I assured Him, "Yes Lord, I love You with all my heart." As if to test me in what I had just spoken, the Holy Spirit asked, "Will you give Me your camera?" By that time, the offering buckets were being passed throughout the congregation. That camera, worth about $1,000 at the time, was precious to me. But I knew that God had spoken to me. As the bucket passed by, I wrote *Canon Elan camera* on a piece of paper and placed it inside.

Expecting a "Well done, good and faithful servant" from the Lord, I was instead further questioned by Him. I was shocked when the Lord asked a second time, "Rob, do you love Me?" I retaliated, "Lord, what do You mean? Didn't I just give You my camera like You asked? I love You with all my heart." He tried me deeper still. "Rob, will you give Me all of your camera equipment?" The words from two years prior rang in my heart, *"You will put down your camera and never pick it up again."*

With a tear in my eye, I pulled out another piece of paper and wrote down a list of all my camera equipment—the portable studio, backdrops, lighting, lenses—at least about $5,000 worth of equipment. I finished writing the list, and whispered, "Yes, Lord, I love You with all my heart." I called for the usher and explained to him that the list belonged with the camera.

Only minutes later, Pastor Gary was giving away items from the offering via the unique means of the Bible Trivia game. He would pull out an item and ask a Bible question. Whoever answered the question correctly received the item. It was a different way of doing things, but it was Spirit-led.

So Pastor Gary was asking questions. People were responding. And items were being given away freely.

Then, Pastor Gary pulled the paper from one of the buckets that had my camera (I mean God's camera) written on it. The people gasped with excitement. Pastor Gary said, "This is a $1,000 camera, and it's here being given away! For this one, I'll ask a very difficult question." I reasoned within myself, *Surely the Lord is testing me like he tested Abraham. He'll return my Isaac to me. I'll know the answer to the question! This must all be a test. I'm going to raise my hand, answer the question and win back what I just sowed. There's no way God is just going to let me give this thing away. This is my career. How am I going to work? Pay my bills?* I visualized myself shooting my hand in the air and shouting, "I know the answer!" I imagined I would win back my equipment and all would be well.

Filled with faith, I already had my hand halfway lifted; I was ready to give the answer.

To this day, I still remember the question.

"Who were the only two men in the Bible to have ever had their wives given away?"

A wave of dread washed over me. I realized, "I don't know the answer."

Pastor Gary scanned the congregation looking for anyone who knew the answer. In the entire crowd, only one person knew it—one lady who was jumping up and down with joy. Pastor Gary called on her. She exclaimed, "The answer is Samson and David!" "You are right!" Pastor Gary announced. "And the camera is here. Who is the person giving away the camera? Both of you join us on the stage, please."

The lady and I both walked onto the stage. She was crying with joy. I was crying with mixed emotions.

Pastor Gary asked me, "Why are you crying?" I was honest, "I'm crying because this is the biggest seed that I have ever sown in my life." The woman told everyone present, "And I am crying because God answers prayers. I am a high school teacher. Every day, as I walk to my class, I pass by the photography room and I lay hands on the door. I asked the Lord to provide me with the best camera equipment possible so that when I go to Mongolia this upcoming summer, I can document the missionary trip. I am going to write about it and take pictures."

It was at that moment that I told her about the rest of the seed I sowed, "God doesn't only want me to give you this camera. He wants me to give you all my camera equipment. You now have the best of the best. Just know that God answers prayer."

Sometimes God will move you prophetically in order for you to sow extravagantly. He'll have you give things away and even be in specific places, because you are a part of His plan. You are a part of the fulfillment of prayers. You have divine appointments to meet. As prophetic people who radically obey the voice of God, we do not only speak prophetic words; we become the prophetic word in action. We cling to nothing but the Lord Himself and recognize that all we possess belongs to the Lord.

But don't think this is the end of my offering story. Peter was asked the question three times: "Do you love Me?" I had only been asked twice. The third time came about a month and a half later. I had already given away my camera and all my equipment, so I had to borrow a camera in order to work. One day while at my job, the voice of the Lord spoke to me again. "Rob, do you love Me?" When I heard the question, all I could do was bow my head and cry. I said, "Lord, You know I love You. I've given everything You've asked of me. I really don't know what more I can give." The words I heard next stopped me in my tracks. The Lord said, "Rob, will you give Me your job?"

My job? *"You will put down your camera and never pick it up again. You will become what you're meant to be, an oracle."*

Without hesitation and before I could talk myself out of it, I finished up my work and drove back to the office. I sat with my boss and told him I would be quitting. My next paycheck was the last one I received from the company.

Now, I don't recommend anyone doing that. But when a person hears the voice of God in the way I did, all I could do was obey. I will admit, it definitely wasn't an easy road I chose to walk. I had just become engaged to Juanita, and there was a wedding to plan. She was finishing up school and only working part-time. My future in-laws went from loving me (my job paid me $60,000 a year) to hating me (I had no income now). How was I supposed to pay for a wedding and begin a new life with Juanita when I had no money?

All I could do was put my faith, hope, and trust in God and in the seed I had sown. If God asked for my camera, my photography equipment, and my job, then He had a plan to take care of me. And He did.

Juanita and I saw miracle after miracle take place for our wedding. Someone purchased our wedding cake. Another person took care of the food for the reception. And another person gave us the money to pay for our honeymoon. Other than little expenses, the main thing we had to pay for was the wedding photographer. *God definitely has a sense of humor.*

This prophetic attribute of radical obedience was something that developed out of a lifestyle of prayer and worship. I was hungry for what God wanted to show me, to hear what He wanted to speak to me. But most importantly, I was hungry for more of God Himself. Spiritual hunger will cause you to do radical things.

HUNGER

As a young prophetic minister, I was driven by a spiritual hunger to seek out mentors and to search for anointed prophets of God. I studied them. I served them. I learned from them. I found one prophet, in particular, to be especially inspiring. His name is Ruckins McKinley. I would often attend his services and assist him.

In my earlier years of ministry, I attended a prophetic conference because I wanted to hear and serve under Ruckins. Even though

Juanita and I were newlyweds at the time and finances were tight, I decided to drive from southern California to northern California just to attend that conference. The drive up to San Jose was about five hours long. I don't know what surprised me more—that my car was able to make the drive or that I was able to afford the gas.

Either way, when I finally arrived at the church where the conference was being held, I was excited. My heart was filled with expectation. I knew that God was going to minister to me in a special way. I stepped out of my car, stretched my legs, and headed toward to church lobby. As I approached, I noticed that the conference attendees were all wearing wristbands. So I went up to one of the check-in tables to get mine. That's when I was told, to my dismay, that there was a fee for the conference. The registration fee was $75 a person. I did not have $75.

So I tried to explain to the conference coordinators, "I am here to assist Prophet Ruckins McKinley. He's one of your main speakers. I am here serving under his ministry. He knows I am coming. He's expecting me." They didn't care. They were adamant about their registration rules. "Nobody gets in unless they're registered. Sorry." They just wouldn't let me in.

Just then, I saw Ruckins walking through the lobby on his way into one of the side rooms where he was about to teach a smaller "breakout" session. I tried to get his attention. "Ruckins!" He saw me and approached. I was relieved to see him. We greeted one another and then I explained the situation. "Ruckins, they're not letting me in even though I told them that I am here to serve your ministry." Ruckins invited me to follow him all the way to the entrance of the side room. That's where we were stopped by the conference staff. Not even Ruckins could get me through the door without a registration.

It was then that Ruckins decided to open a window inside the small conference room. He told me to go outside so that I could watch the session from the window. It was the only way that he was able to get me involved in the meeting.

So there I stood, outside of the window of a small conference room. I did not have a chair. It was hot, and I didn't have the luxury of air conditioning. My only relief was found in the shade of a single tree. I literally just stood there as Ruckins and two other prophets ministered. They ministered for over two hours. The first two prophets who ministered merely glanced at me before continuing with their ministry to the people inside the building. They didn't even give me a second glance, because I wasn't in the room.

But Prophet Ruckins saw something in me that the others did not. When he looked at me, when he looked at my situation, the prophet saw hunger, godly desire, and pure zeal. Suddenly the prophet leaned himself outside of the window, reaching out toward me, and he grabbed me by the back of the neck. He shouted, "Everything

I have within me, I impart to you!" And he released the prophetic anointing into my life.

There was no catcher standing behind me, and I wasn't standing on cushy church carpet. There was nothing there to soften the impact of my fall, but I felt the power of God go through me. I hit the concrete, and I remained there until the end of the service. I stayed there until God finished imparting into me everything He desired to impart. That was a significant day in my spiritual journey.

When you hunger for something, you do not let the word *no* stop you. When you burn with the prophetic fire, you are an unstoppable blaze that dashes through the brush of fear and obstacles. Radical obedience, fueled by godly hunger, pushes you beyond the limitations of fear, delay, and obstruction. In fact, when you have a prophetic mantle on your life, it's difficult to settle for anything less than radical obedience toward God's commands.

Jeremiah, no longing wanting to speak the word of the Lord because of the consequences, was unable to stifle the voice of God for long.

> *When I speak, the words burst out. "Violence and destruction!" I shout. So these messages from the Lord have made me a household joke. But if I say I'll never mention the Lord or speak in his name, his word burns in my heart like a fire. It's like a fire in my bones! I am worn out trying to hold it in! I can't do it!* (Jeremiah 20:8-9)

When you are disobedient to what God asks you to do, it makes you miserable. There's no use in holding back anyway. No matter what others say, no matter what it costs you, no matter how long it takes, radically obey what God has clearly spoken.

Notes on Your Prophetic Journey

Notes on Your Prophetic Journey

CHAPTER 3

WORSHIP

HOW I MET MY WIFE

Summer, 1995. I was traveling with a worship ministry team, serving in whatever capacity they needed. One day we were ministering at a church in San Jose, California, and the church's worship singers were on the stage. The people were ministering to the Lord at the altar. In the midst of my praising God, I was blindsided by the word of the Lord. The Lord spoke so clearly to me, and I was certain of it. I wasn't exactly looking for a word. My focus was on worshiping God. Nevertheless, God audibly—yes, audibly—spoke to me saying, "Rob, look up. Within two weeks, you and Becky will be no more, and one from this worship team will become your wife."

Becky, a young lady I was dating, was there in that service too, yet I felt the pull that I had to look, though discreetly, at my future wife. As I glanced at the singers on the stage, I took note of all the ladies on the team. All of them were married, with the exception of two. Of course, God was not drawing my attention to any of the married women. So I zeroed in on the other two as I discerned. Of the two women remaining, one woman spoke only Spanish. I didn't speak Spanish, so, by the process of elimination, I came to focus my eyes on one beautiful woman—Juanita. I thought to myself, *Can this really be?*

But that word stuck with me. I couldn't get it out of my mind.

Later, I approached one of my ministry mentors—her name was Rebecca. I said, "Rebecca, God spoke to me when I was at the altar."

Interested, Rebecca pressed, "Really? What did He say?"

I was somewhat shy about telling her, but I did, "Well, He said that I would marry someone from this church, from the worship team. And I just can't shake that word. I'm certain it's God."

Rebecca paused to reflect for a moment. She encouraged me, "Rob, you hear God's voice clearer than anyone I know. Just hold on to it, and let's see what God does."

And hold on to it I certainly did. Juanita and I are now happily married.

It was during a time of worship that I clearly heard the Lord regarding my future wife, and it is during worship that I connect with Heaven in a way that brings forth a strong prophetic flow. Worship puts one's mind on God, and a mind focused on God allows for one's spirit to see and hear clearly. Worship is essential to the prophetic ministry and lifestyle. In worship, you will find a certain clarity that is difficult to obtain by any other means.

If you are going to flow in your full prophetic potential, you must learn to worship.

WORSHIP

The simple meaning of the word *worship* is to fall down prostrate before the Lord; to pay homage, respect, to adore, or to be reverential toward.

Worship is the magnification of God in the midst of forgetting oneself. It is to look at God with a heart full of adoration and awe, and it is a powerful act—I would even call it a state of being. When you take the posture of reverence in the presence of God, that posture allows you to hear the Spirit of God as He comes forth in the voice of the Father.

Worship positions you to hear clearly in the Spirit. A mind that is set on worship is so obsessed with God that it gives virtually no attention to anything else. Worship takes you away to the High Place; it breaks you free from earthly bounds, and allows you to soar. At those spiritual heights, it's easy to begin hearing God.

In the church world today, there are many who praise but few who can truly worship. Praise gives thanks for what God has done, but worship adores God for who He is. Praise comes from the will, but worship comes from the spirit, your inner man. I've seen believers dance during praise songs, but the minute the hush of the glory comes into the room, they twiddle their thumbs in boredom. I find it amazing that a people so excited over the idea of God's goodness can so quickly shift to an apathetic posture.

When you experience what God has done, you praise, but when you catch a glimpse of who God is, you worship. Only worshipers are moved by the Spirit of prophecy, because only worshipers walk in an intimacy with God. Intimacy and worship feed into one another. Worship causes God to reveal more of Himself to you, and that revelation causes you to worship.

Notes on Your Prophetic Journey

Notes on Your Prophetic Journey

CHAPTER 4

THE SEEMINGLY STRANGE

AUTUMN

I was ministering at a church in Washington State. The prophetic was so clear that I was able to call people out by name. During that sensational time of ministry, I was moved in my spirit to call out someone by the name of Autumn. The uniqueness of that name struck me. I called out, "Autumn, are you here? Raise your hand. Let me know if you are here."

There were probably about 150 people in the church building. As I looked over the crowd, there was an expectant pause. Nobody raised their hand. Trying to find Autumn, the people began to look around—their heads turning back and forth as they searched. I knew that God had spoken to me, but nobody was responding.

I persisted, "I have this name, it's so strong in my spirit. I must pray for you, Autumn." Still, nobody signaled me. A bit perplexed, I settled for, "Is anyone here perhaps praying for an Autumn?" My question was met only with more silence, but I knew that God had given me that name. I was definitely supposed to minister a prophetic word to an Autumn. I decided to let it go for the time being. I told the people, "Well, I am going to move forward and keep ministering to other people. But I'll keep praying for Autumn. I believe Autumn is here."

I moved on and began to minister to others. But the Lord wouldn't let me forget about Autumn. After speaking only a few other prophetic words over people, I again began to search for Autumn. "Autumn, are you here? I can feel you. If you are here, raise your hand." I think that at that point, the people thought I had missed it, because still nobody responded.

Not wanting to miss my prophetic assignment, I finally just said to myself, "Lord, show me Autumn." I continued to minister to others, but as I did I moved around the building.

Eventually, I found myself standing in front of a young woman. She couldn't have been more than 23 or 24 years old. She was wearing a lot of makeup and she looked dejected, downcast. I moved the microphone away from my mouth, looked the young girl in the eyes, and said, "Autumn?"

She reluctantly explained, "That's not my name. Well, that's not my real name. It's my stage name. I'm a dancer."

I responded, "Well, Autumn, the Lord has sent me here to deliver you. You will live and not die. I see the suicide letter that you have written, but even if you take those pills, you will not die. The Lord has sent me to save you and to deliver you from the lie."

As the prophetic word was being spoken over her, she began to weep and cry. She laid her head on my shoulder, and I began to pray that God would deliver her from oppression and sadness, that God would spare her life. When she picked her head up, she had left a fair amount of makeup on my shirt. When she noticed what she had done, she looked mortified and cried, "Oh, I am so sorry!"

I replied, "Autumn, this is the greatest gift you could have ever given me." You see, in my eyes, her tears represented her deliverance. Looking at her again, I declared, "Autumn, hear me. You will live and not die."

She then confided, "My family has rejected me, and I feel like I have nothing to live for. I tried to make ends meet as a dancer. I just came to church this morning to ask God for forgiveness."

I prayed over her and declared life to her. She had already written the suicide note that morning before service, and even though she received the word, she still tried to commit suicide later that day, hours after the service. And although she had put the plan in motion, God foiled her plans. I was told later that Autumn lived.

A season for a name—it seemed strange to most of the people in attendance, but God knew what would get her attention. Prophetic revelation will reveal details about people's lives that are so specific that they seem odd to others. But those little details, personal touches the Spirit puts on each ministering declaration, add to the weight of what is being said. Often, the seemingly strange is where the power is the greatest. These peculiar words—because they are so personal—can be the most memorable.

FREEDOM FROM A FROG

In 2001, I was visiting the United States Penitentiary in Florence, Colorado. I was holding special prophetic meetings for the inmates. During one of the services, I received a prophetic unction and prophesied, "There's somebody here who's been so addicted to a high of drugs that you have gone out to find a frog, and you've been licking that frog. And God wants to set you free."

As I called out that prophetic word, a man responded. He was small in stature, wore glasses, and had blond, wavy hair. He carried himself with a certain frailty. He waved at me and said, "That's me! I want to be free."

When I laid hands on him, I felt the power of God rush through my body. The power of the Holy Spirit instantly set that man free from that addiction.

The man later revealed that he had kept a Colorado Horny Toad in captivity. The man would squeeze the toad causing it to release a toxic secretion. He would then lick the secretion for a high. The man compared the high to an acid trip.

Right after the meeting, he and a few of his friends released the frog.

Had I not been keen to hearing the voice of God, I would have thought, *A frog? That's random. I doubt that means anything significant. This must just be my own thought.* If we're not willing to embrace the strange and the random, we will miss many powerful prophetic moments. I wonder how many times we've missed divine appointments simply because we ignored the stranger prophetic unctions.

TAIWANESE GOVERNMENT

In 2012, during some of my ministry meetings in Taiwan, a high-ranking government official came to see me minister. The man told me that he had a friend, who also worked for the government, whom he wanted me to meet. So I was taken to a government facility where I met with both men.

I sat there, listening to them speak to one another in their native language. I couldn't understand a word they were saying. However, judging by their tone, I was able to surmise that there was some sort of minor conflict or point of disagreement between the two of them.

The man who had come to my meeting was trying to convince his friend to be receptive to me. The friend was very skeptical. He was a believer, but he did not believe in prophets; he also believed that men shouldn't be given titles. He did not believe that I could see into the future or hear from God. So he was not very open to hearing from me.

After arguing for several minutes, the skeptical man looked at me and said, in English, "If you are a prophet, tell me what I said to my wife last night."

Under the prophetic anointing, I ministered to the man. As I shared my vision with him, I held up my fists close together as if I were handcuffed. I told him, "Well, I had a vision of you. And I see you holding your hands together in front of your wife saying, 'I am tired of being handcuffed. I am tired of having my hands tied. I accepted this position in government because I wanted to make a difference for God's Kingdom. But they keep blocking me. They do not allow me to do what I need to do.'"

I continued, "And you told your wife that you were going to retire, but the word of the Lord to you is that it is not your season to leave government. God has put you here with a purpose and has destined great things for Taiwan. You will be a major part of it."

The man was amazed at how I heard his words and even saw his hand gestures in the Spirit. He went from being a skeptic to being completely open. He admitted, "That's exactly what I spoke to my wife last night. Nobody knows that but her. I am frustrated because I am being prevented from doing what's in my heart to do." As he began to cry, he called for an administrator to enter the room. The official spoke something to his administrator, then the administrator walked out. He returned after several minutes with something in his hand, which he handed to the man.

The official gave me what was called "The Hat of Favor." Because I wore that hat, I was honored everywhere I went in that government facility. When they saw that hat, the people would stop and bow in reverence. The hat represented favor from someone of importance. He gave me many other gifts as a sign of honor, but what brought me the most joy was this fact: A man who was once filled with doubt had become filled with faith.

When you know the voice of God, you can be instructed to say and do odd things. Who would have ever thought that pretending to be handcuffed could change someone else's perspective in life? But those who do strange things in obedience are also favored. Rejoice in the peculiarity. In the scripture, prophets did strange things all the time. You are among God's great company.

Isaiah the prophet wandered around prophesying naked for three years.

> *Then the Lord said, "My servant Isaiah has been walking around naked and barefoot for the last three years. This is a sign—a symbol of the terrible troubles I will bring upon Egypt and Ethiopia"* (Isaiah 20:3).

At the command of God, Hosea the prophet married a prostitute.

> *When the Lord first began speaking to Israel through Hosea, he said to him, "Go and marry a prostitute, so that some of her children will be conceived in prostitution. This will illustrate how Israel has acted like a prostitute by turning against the Lord and worshiping other gods"* (Hosea 1:2).

Ezekiel was commanded to cook a meal over human waste.

> *Prepare and eat this food as you would barley cakes. While all the people are watching, bake it over a fire using dried human dung as fuel and then eat the bread* (Ezekiel 4:12).

Of course, you must be careful. You shouldn't just do and say anything that randomly comes into your mind. But when God speaks to you, when you know His voice, be obedient. Say and do as He says. It's okay to be a little different. After all, you are prophetic.

Notes on Your Prophetic Journey

Notes on Your Prophetic Journey

CHAPTER 5

RESTORATION

THE COLOMBIAN GOVERNOR

While ministering in Colombia, I was introduced to a high-ranking government official, through the connections of a pastor friend of mine, in the city of Medellín. I was taken to the official's office where the man was carrying on with his regular work tasks.

My pastor friend spoke in Spanish with the official for several minutes. With prophetic insight already revealing the man's secrets, I sat there patiently and watched them speak to one another. The pastor explained to the official about me, "This is a man of God. He has the wisdom to hear from Heaven and speak it into your life. God speaks through him."

The official was a religious man, but he was not at all familiar with the prophetic or the work of the Holy Spirit. I could tell that he was a little skeptical but open. Finally, he looked right into my eyes and asked, "What would God have to say to me?"

I gave him the word of the Lord and said, "When I looked at you, I could see that you have been living in regret for seven years. I do not mean to offend you, but seven years ago, you had an affair—you cheated on your wife. Also, I can see you groaning in pain, because you've seen your daughter grow up without you really being there. You regret that you've put so much time into your work and your political office. But nobody knows that you've been secretly dating your ex-wife. You have been believing, praying, and asking God to restore your marriage. You recognize your mistake and want restoration. God is going to repair your marriage."

The official pressed his face into his desk and began to weep. With tears on his face, he explained, "Nobody knows this." He pointed to his security guards and told me, "Not even they know this. But this is all true. My ex-wife and I have been dating. Last night, we were talking about being remarried."

The word of the Lord confirmed the hope within that man. It brought restoration where there was devastation.

The prophetic is a powerful gift from God. Not only does it make people aware of God's voice and heart, it has the power to set restoration into motion. Because of the word that Colombian political official received, he had the courage to move forward—he received confirmation from God about the direction of his life.

The Spirit of God's power is on you when you prophesy. It can bring restoration for people because of the power of God that your words contain.

SKEPTIC IN HOUSTON

I prayed for a woman in Houston, Texas. She had just been in a terrible car accident and had come to the service believing for a miracle in her body. Her arm was severely broken. The doctors surgically screwed five metal plates into her hand. The prognosis was tragic—that she would live with pain for the rest of her life and never again have full mobility in her hand.

While praying for her healing, I prophesied, "God is going to take away your pain, and the doctors will be amazed when full mobility is restored to your hand." Immediately, the pain left her hand. She began to scream, cry, and move her hand freely.

Just then, I noticed that the woman's teenage daughter, who had also been in the accident but was uninjured, did not look very impressed. The look on her face said, "Mom, you always overreact. You are exaggerating."

Seeing the skepticism on the daughter, I began to prophesy. Instantly, I received a vision. In the vision, I was in the daughter's room.

Disclosing details about the young woman's room that I had no way of knowing outside of prophetic revelation, I spoke: "I see your room is a mess. You know it is, but you don't want to clean it. You don't have the motivation to clean it because you are in a place of deep depression. The last time your mother asked you to clean your room, you took all of the clean clothes that she gave you and you just went and stuffed them into the closet. I hear the Lord saying, 'The other day, you had a thought about cleaning your closet. That wasn't just your thought—that was Me.'"

The young woman was no longer scoffing at the prophetic. Now, she was glued to every word. I continued to talk about her cleaning her closet, but there was a deeper meaning behind what I was speaking, because there was a deeper reason why she lacked the motivation to do so. "You went and opened your closet door. The first words you said were, 'I don't even know where to begin.' It was the Holy Spirit who was nudging you to clean and rearrange. You began to weep, and you said, 'I don't know how.'"

Just then, the young woman looked at her mom and asked, "How does he know this?"

I explained, "It's the Lord. He's revealing things to me. The reason why He wants you to clean your closet is because your closet is a symbol of your heart. As you clean your closet, it will be a prophetic reflection of what's happening within you. By faith, clean it. God will clean your heart. You'll no longer be angry with your father. You'll no longer despise men. You'll learn to love."

Just then with her permission, I acted as a prophetic stand-in, as a father figure, and kissed her on the crown of her head. God used me to release the power of the Father's kiss. The word *kiss* means to equip, to outfit, or to overcome. In that moment, the Spirit of affirmation fell upon her. She fell to the floor and soaked in the presence of God.

RESTORATION

What that struggling girl had lacked in love, affirmation, and joy, the Father's touch restored through a prophetic act of affection.

When Israel was experiencing agricultural disaster, the word of the Lord came to the prophet Joel. He prophesied a restoration of rain, grain, and grapes. He prophesied a time of refreshing and restoration.

> *Rejoice, you people of Jerusalem! Rejoice in the Lord your God! For the rain he sends demonstrates his faithfulness. Once more the autumn rains will come, as well as the rains of spring. The threshing floors will again be piled high with grain, and the presses will overflow with new wine and olive oil* (Joel 2:23-24).

Like the prophet Joel, God has sent you to declare restoration wherever you step foot. Where you see lack, declare abundance. Where you see dismay, declare joy. Where you see disaster, prophesy order. You have been given the prophetic power to speak restoration over the men and women you encounter.

Notes on Your Prophetic Journey

Notes on Your Prophetic Journey

CHAPTER 6

HEALING

THE CRITTER MIRACLE

In 1999 or so, I was ministering at a church called Praise Chapel in Huntington Park, California. During the prophetic ministry, I received a word of knowledge. The Lord spoke to me and said, "You must pray for Critter."

I began to tell the congregation, "I need to pray for Critter. Who's Critter? What's going on? I need to pray for someone named Critter. I have a word from the Lord. His life is in danger."

It turns out that "Critter" was a nickname for a young man in that church who, unknown to him, had sugar diabetes. At the time I was ministering, he was in the hospital in a diabetic coma. He was engaged to be married, but the doctors did not expect him to live.

I prophesied, "In three days, Critter will suddenly wake up out of the coma, and he will be well. He will live and not die."

That was on a Friday. On Sunday, Critter awoke from his coma.

When life hangs in the balance and hope is not to be found, God sends forth His prophets to bring life to the circumstance. Even the dead can hear the authority in a prophetic declaration, and they respond according to what God has spoken. Even sickness must obey the true divine ordinances of God's chosen vessels, the prophets. As you speak the declarations and proclamations of God, and as you speak edification, exhortation, and comfort, God will breathe His life into people and awaken them from their slumber.

GRAND SLAM

I received a phone call from a good friend. As soon as he began to speak, I could hear the stress and worry in his voice. Over the phone, he explained to me that during a baseball game, his son suffered a significant knee injury—a torn PCL and meniscus—and was carted off the baseball field by a medical team. The damage was so great that the doctors pronounced that his son's baseball season was over.

"Please, pray for my son," my friend requested.

That's when the word of the Lord came to me concerning his son. "It's not as it seems. There will be no swelling in the leg, and you will need to get a second opinion." After sharing that word, I went over to pray for the boy in person.

Right then and there, God healed the boy completely. When I first arrived, the boy was taking pain pills and walking on crutches. After we prayed, he began walking pain-free, and he became a demonstration of God's power to heal.

Within two weeks, he was medically cleared to get back on the baseball field. There was no trace of the tear in his PCL or meniscus. But that wasn't the end of it.

The word of the Lord came to me again. This time, the Lord spoke a blessing on top of the healing. I prophesied, "God is going to end your college baseball career with an exclamation point."

On his final at bat of his senior season, he came up with the bases loaded and hit a grand slam. The Lord not only healed him, but placed an exclamation point on his college baseball career.

Now here's what I find interesting. The doctors had determined that the boy had suffered a career-ending injury. But after we prayed, there was not a single trace of a tear; it was like he had never been injured. This result was beyond just a healing (though miraculous healing is powerful in and of itself); this was the prophetic rolling back the clock.

There's something to be said of the prophetic ministry and how it relates to time. It can transport you into someone's past, where you witness specific details of an event that took place. It can also take you to the future and allow you to bring some of the future back with you. You can catch a glimpse of God's plan—what He would like to accomplish in someone's life.

When it came to that boy's baseball injury, the prophetic anointing brought forth healing by making it so that the injury simply never was. The prophetic ministry is a healing ministry.

MARI'S MIRACLE

Years ago, I prophesied the birth of a girl named Mari. As Mari grew into a beautiful little girl, she developed alopecia, a disease that caused her hair to fall out rapidly—often in chunks. Making plans to help Mari cope with the disease, the doctors offered Mari's parents, Jose and Angela, the option of using a wig to hide her baldness. Concerned for their daughter's well-being, Jose and Angela wondered what to do next. They considered the wig but believed for a miracle.

But little Mari, calm and full of faith, said, "Mommy, all we have to do is call the prophet, and when prophet Rob prays for me, my hair will be healed."

So, in response to her faith, Jose and Angela allowed Mari to call me. When I heard the news about her diagnosis, I thought about the reality that God did not give Mari long, wavy, beautiful hair just so that it could fall out. Over the phone, I prophesied over Mari and prayed for her hair.

Three months later, Mari went in for a checkup. The doctors were amazed at what they saw. All of Mari's bald spots were completely covered. Her hair had regrown. In fact, her hair that had fallen out regrew to the exact same length as the rest of her hair. There wasn't a trace of alopecia to see.

Again with Mari's miracle, it becomes apparent that the prophetic anointing can work divine healing in the physical bodies of those who receive a prophetic word or prayer—and in a way that defies time constraints.

HOLE IN THE FACE

Sometimes sickness is tied to a spiritual root. Often, the scripture tells of how Jesus would cast out demons and heal the sick simultaneously. You can see the connection between sickness and the spiritual in this verse:

> *One day Jesus cast out a demon from a man who couldn't speak, and when the demon was gone, the man began to speak. The crowds were amazed* (Luke 11:14).

Thankfully, the prophetic has the power to remove sickness at its root.

For example, I was ministering in Bogotá, Colombia prophesying to multitudes of people over a series of several services. A woman, who came from a prominent Colombian family, visited one of the services. The woman was a dentist, and sadly she was also demonically oppressed and tormented. She lived with constant demonic harassment. The demonic beings that tormented her would influence her to do bizarre things.

In one instance, disturbed to the point of extreme frustration, the woman had taken a blunt drill and intentionally punctured her own face. She made a hole that went all the way through her face—the drill was pressed through every layer of skin. Her injury was so severe that seven plastic surgeons refused to operate on her. According to them, it was not possible to close the hole and, more than likely, she would eventually develop skin cancer. I don't know exactly why the surgeons were so limited in their ability to treat her properly, but that poor woman was forced to wear a mask in order to cover the hole.

The demon-oppressed woman heard about the service through a friend, who happened to be a pastor. She was told that there was a prophet from America who would be able to pray for her and help her. Under the supervision of her family, the woman attended the service.

I remember praying over her. I could feel the intense inner turmoil. She was so fearful, so disturbed by forces of darkness. I began to prophesy over her, "God is healing you. There is something you carry in your heart. You can't forgive yourself. There's something you can't forgive yourself for." Just then, the heavens were opened, and I saw a child in the heavens. When I told the woman that I was seeing a child, she began to cry. As she trembled and wept, I could see her being set free. Her tears were tears of deliverance.

It turns out, the woman had an abortion in the past. Since the day of her decision, she had become depressed. The enemy took advantage of an already grieving woman and attached himself to her grief. I declared, "You are free from this heaviness." In that moment, her heavy weight of depression was lifted.

By the next morning, God had done for that woman what seven plastic surgeons were unable to do. In one night, God healed what would have taken men months to heal. When the woman woke up, not only was she free of her depression, she was free from demonic torment and guilt. And—she was completely healed. The hole in her face had closed.

THE PROPHETIC AND DIVINE HEALING

Let God also flow through you as you prophesy and minister to suffering people. The power of the prophetic is in the declaration. You have been given the authority to command sickness to flee. Think of Elisha the prophet, who didn't even have to lay hands on Naaman in order for him to be healed of leprosy. Elisha simply spoke a word.

> *But Elisha sent a messenger out to him with this message: "Go and wash yourself seven times in the Jordan River. Then your skin will be restored, and you will be healed of your leprosy"* (2 Kings 5:10).

Though Naaman became upset at the word, it didn't diminish the power or truth of the word that was spoken. You need to understand that people won't always like the words you give, but don't let that hinder you from ministering to people. By you giving the word, it activates the Spirit of God within the word to work and accomplish what it needs.

The prophetic can also get down into the depths of the human soul in order to deal directly with the root to which a sickness has attached itself. You can speak as far as you can see, and because the basis of the prophetic gift is the word of God, it can see deep into people.

> *For the word of God is alive and powerful. It is sharper than the sharpest two-edged sword, cutting between soul and spirit, between joint and marrow. It exposes our innermost thoughts and desires* (Hebrews 4:12).

So be certain of this—wherever the prophetic flows, healing can also flow.

Notes on Your Prophetic Journey

Notes on Your Prophetic Journey

CHAPTER 7

HEAVEN IS OPEN

THE HAUNTED CLINIC

Religious people will *dislike* this story, and religious spirits will *hate* this story. But I love that the prophetic dismantles religious philosophy.

I was asked to pay a visit to a medical clinic for the purpose of performing a deliverance on the building. Pray deliverance over a building? I had never really done such a thing before, but the person who contacted me was adamant that I go and pray over the clinic.

Apparently, patients and staff were troubled by the sound of a baby crying. The sound of a baby crying can make people uncomfortable, yes; but this was supernatural in nature. You see, there were no children or babies present in the clinic. The crying they heard was coming from seemingly nowhere. Patients would often run out of the building, freaked out by the unexplained cries.

Of course, I knew the source of the terrifying sounds. What the world calls "ghosts" and "the paranormal," we the Church call "demonic."

When I arrived at the clinic, I began to pray. It was then that I received a vision. In that vision, I saw a man who I knew, by the Spirit, was a freemason. As I was in the Spirit and in the spiritual realm, the Lord revealed to me what was taking place.

I explained to the staff what was being revealed to me from the Lord, "The former owner of this medical building was a freemason. He would 'help' the elders of his lodge by secretly aborting their unwanted babies conceived in extra-marital affairs."

Later researching my claim, one of the doctors confirmed that the former owner of the building was, in fact, a freemason. I am sure you know that, after we prayed, the "paranormal" sounds of babies crying were never again heard in that clinic. The clinic was delivered from demonic influence.

But before I left the clinic, the owner asked me to pray for one of her staff members in particular. As the owner was making this special prayer request, she motioned her hand toward a young lady who was approaching. The moment I looked at that young lady, the prophetic in me was stirred. Without leaving a moment for greetings and introductions, I began to prophesy. The next words out of my mouth were, "Premature death will no longer happen in your family."

Just then, I looked upward and was able to see into the heavens. I am telling you—it was an open vision. I saw two people standing there in the heavens. I knew by the Spirit of prophecy that the two people I saw were related to that young lady. I could sense the strong connection. In the spiritual realm, connections between people are strongly felt, but it is difficult to describe what that connection feels like. But again, I knew that the two men were relatives of the young lady.

I revealed, "I see two people standing in glory. They are two men. One of them is your uncle, and I see that he died of a heart problem. The other man is your cousin, and I see that he passed away in a horrific, tragic car accident."

I looked back at the young lady. Her wide, teary eyes were locked on to me. She trembled as she placed her hand over her mouth. I repeated, "God says that premature death will no longer happen in your family. It will never happen again." I was further inspired to instruct, "And you need to go tell your auntie that her son is not in hell like the preacher said."

There in that clinic, the young lady began to weep in a way that moved everyone around her. You could feel the Holy Spirit working in the atmosphere. God further pressed upon me, "And to confirm that what I am saying is truly from God, to prove to your aunt that I've seen her son in Heaven, I will describe who I saw. He is about five feet, nine inches in height. He has wavy hair, an olive complexion, and brightly colored eyes. And he was known on the earth as a smiley man. Go tell his mother that her son is not in hell."

The young lady rejoiced as she explained, "I know that was my cousin you saw, because you described him exactly, and his nick-name was 'Smiley'; everyone called him 'Smiley.'"

Struggling to speak while fighting through her tears, the young lady revealed that, at the time of his accident, her cousin had been caught up doing the wrong things with the wrong people. The preacher, implying an ill fate, told the mother, "Hopefully he had a chance to repent just before he was killed." Because of those words, the mother was living in guilt and torment. The thought of her child in hell agonized her. She was convinced that her son was in hell. She lived this way until the word of the Lord came to set her free.

A religious spirit tormented that poor mother. It attached itself to her mind because of a religious suggestion from a religious man. Religious spirits do not like stories like the one I just shared with you. They hate that God used a so-called "haunted clinic" to set a family up for deliverance. They hate that I was able to see into Heaven—because they do not want Heaven on earth. They'd rather Heaven be an abstract, distant idea. They hate that someone they would deem as hell-bound would be caught and saved by the hand of grace.

But you need to know something—the heavens are open. In fact, that was neither the first nor the last time I saw into Heaven in such a way.

IT'S NOT YOUR FAULT

Prophesying at a church in Washington State, I called out a young man who looked tired. I do not mean that he looked like he had no sleep; I mean that he looked like he had no peace. When I called him forward, the heavens were opened, and I saw a woman. I told the young man, "I see a lady standing in the heavens. I hear her saying these words: 'Son, it's not your fault; you are forgiven.' I believe it's your mother."

As if he had held in his emotions for years, he began to cry—a good hard cry. The moment he heard those words, it was like something broke off of him. He pressed his hand over his eyes, slightly bent over, and cried so much that he shook.

Eventually, he regained some of his composure and explained, "You have no idea. The only one who truly knows the way that I feel is my wife. I have lived with guilt for years because I had to put my mother into a home. My son is autistic, and I wasn't able to care for both of them at the same time. That's why I had to put her in a home. Shortly after I put her into a home, she passed away. For so long,

I've carried this burden—I felt like it was my fault that she died. I've lived with the guilt."

Because of the word of the Lord, the guilt was lifted from his shoulders. When a prophet stands under an open Heaven, he or she can call down grace and forgiveness.

MAMA, I FORGIVE YOU

Irvine, California—the year was 2017. I was ministering at a church service when I began to prophesy over a woman. A flash of multiple visions arrested my attention. I saw violent images, guns, drugs, alcohol, and chaos. In an instant, God revealed to me what it all meant. I opened my mouth, "Ma'am, you are the kind of woman whom God is going to use to go into the pits and into the dark places. You are going to be a rescuer. You are going to pull women out of abuse and into safety. God is using you to deliver women out of abusive relationships and out of unsafe environments."

The Holy Spirit quickened me and drew my attention to a second woman. She was standing two rows in front of the first woman I was prophesying over. I pointed at her and declared, "And you are one of the women whom God has rescued through that woman I was just prophesying to. As a matter of fact, she was on assignment to deliver you from the hands of an abusive man. Also, I hear three voices from Heaven all saying, 'Mama, I forgive you. Mama, I forgive you.' And

I see three babies—two boys and a girl. They're each saying, 'Mama, I forgive you. It's time to move forward. Forgive yourself.'"

The second woman wept and trembled.

After the service, she came up to me and poured out her heart. She expressed her deep-felt guilt, "You have no idea, Prophet, how right you are! I have three babies in Heaven."

I added, "Yes, because you aborted them."

She wept again, "Yes, and I've lived in torment. I have seven children, but I should have ten."

I interjected, "I know the reason you aborted them was because you were raped."

She affirmed, "But I know the Word of God. It doesn't make a difference. I shouldn't have done it. I know that God would have blessed those babies. And I know that every baby has a purpose. I just can't convince myself to move on. I just can't forgive myself for what I've done. My life is stuck. I am living under the weight of drug abuse, unhealthy relationships, and violence—I know it all comes back to this guilt."

I assured her, "But God has set you free from that guilt today. Remember, I heard your children say, 'Mama, I forgive you.'"

She wept some more as she received her deliverance.

THE CYCLE OF INTIMACY

How is it that I, in those prophetic moments, can see into the heavens? How does a prophet position himself or herself under that sort of divine opening and receive visions? The heavens are always open, but it takes a prophet who walks in intimacy with God to access them.

Prophecy is always birthed through an intimate relationship with God. Therefore, the Spirit of prophecy and worship are knitted together—they are both marks of intimacy. You can become caught in a beautiful cycle of closeness with God.

Revelation inspires worship. Worship initiates intimacy. Intimacy yields revelation.

And as you continually loop through that cycle, prophecy begins to flow out of you. So if worship is the key to intimacy and revelation is the key to worship, then where does one go to find the revelation that will begin the spiritual movement?

The answer is the Word. The Word is divine. When you get into the Word, you are gazing into an open heaven.

The Word brings forth revelation. That revelation inspires worship. That worship brings intimacy. That intimacy empowers prophecy. But it begins with the Word. As you are faithful with the revelation that God has already made available to you, you position yourself to hear more from Him.

> *To those who listen to my teaching, more understanding will be given, and they will have an abundance of knowledge. But for those who are not listening, even what little understanding they have will be taken away from them* (Matthew 13:12).

I cannot tell you how many times someone has come up to me and said, "Prophet, I need a word" or "Prophet, do you have a word for me?" Of course, if God moves me to share what I see on or in someone, I share it. But I am not always comfortable with people trying to create their own prophetic moment. There's a fine line between spiritual hunger and manipulation.

So sometimes, when someone says, "Prophet Rob, does God have a word for me?" I simply say, "Yes, many—in the Bible."

When I am backed into an awkward corner like that, I like to point people to the Word. Too often, believers get lazy. They want a word from a prophet, but they do not ever open the Bible for themselves. I find that it's usually the diligent believer who receives the *now word* of the Lord. Why? Because they've stewarded well the revelation that God has already given to them—so God trusts them with more.

Of course, God can do anything He wants, and prophecy is for everyone. But generally speaking, that's how the Lord works.

If you want the spirit of prophecy to flow through you at full power, then you absolutely need to be in the Word. The Word and worship bring forth intimacy.

If you do not have the knowledge of God's Word in your spirit, you can't give it forth. So all prophecy really springs forth from relationship.

Intimacy with God is the prophetic lifestyle—intimacy through worship and the Word. When you live in such a spiritual state of intimacy, you are walking in continual harmony with God. Perhaps you are looking for that harmony. Maybe you have a pull toward the prophetic but feel as though you are living in chaos.

The reality is that if you learn how to step back, you will see God step forward. Taking the time for intimacy with God is first and foremost. Allow God's Spirit to manifest over circumstances and situations. Take time for the Word and worship. The Word is truth, and worship is the key to intimacy—so this verse is one a prophetic person should commit to memory:

> *God is Spirit, and those who worship Him must worship in spirit and truth* (John 4:24 NKJV).

To worship God, to walk in intimacy with your Father, you need both spirit and truth. When we begin to understand the power of intimacy, we begin to enter into greater dimensions with Christ. And in those greater dimensions, the line between heaven and you begins to thin. You don't just gaze into an open heaven; you become an open heaven. Just as God can pour out His Spirit through an open heaven, you also become a vessel God can flow through.

Notes on Your Prophetic Journey

Notes on Your Prophetic Journey

CHAPTER 8

DELIVERANCE FROM THE DEMONIC

HEAD-BUTT IN OREGON

While walking through the congregation and ministering in the prophetic at a church in Oregon, I noticed a certain man. Naturally speaking, there was nothing especially distinct about him. I simply noticed him. When you live in the prophetic anointing, often, you'll be drawn to certain individuals for varying reasons—they just stand out. It's like God highlights them.

I walked up to the man and extended my hand to greet him. As we shook hands, I smiled at him and simply said, "Good to meet you." Within seconds, his demeanor changed from pleasant to aggressive. His face contorted with rage as his grip on my hand tightened. "What are you doing?" I asked. He growled, sneered, and began to crush my hand. He was trying to harm me physically. It was clear to me, and likely to most in the room, that the man was demon-possessed.

A boldness overwhelmed me as I commanded, "In the name of Jesus, be free!" And as I took authority over that evil spirit, I head-butted the man. Yes, you read that correctly. I jerked my forehead against his.

But God's power was added to my head-butt. The power of God struck that man the moment I struck him. The man flew backward about five feet, crashed onto the floor, and remained on the floor for the remainder of the service. I knew by the Spirit that he was instantly delivered.

He approached me after the service with only one thing to say: "I feel so free."

The prophetic mantle on your life will force issues and matters to the surface. It does the same thing with demonic powers. When a prophetic person enters a room, the atmosphere changes. And in that atmosphere, the things within, both good and evil, are forced into the light. The very same thing happened to Jesus. Often, Jesus would cause demons to manifest merely by His approach or nearness.

> *So they brought the boy. But when the evil spirit saw Jesus, it threw the child into a violent convulsion, and he fell to the ground, writhing and foaming at the mouth* (Mark 9:20).

In the presence of a prophetic anointing, demonic beings are not only exposed, they are expelled.

NEVER AGAIN

I was attending a prophetic conference in Zion, Illinois. At the Sunday morning service, which was the last service of the conference, I wore my Sunday best—a suit and tie. The atmosphere was what you'd expect from a prophetic conference; it was charged with power. People carried themselves with both dignity and expectation. When the service ended, I joined all the conference attendees in the foyer to say my goodbyes. I shook some hands, gave some hugs, and then I began to make my way downstairs to the fellowship hall, where all the ministers were gathering for lunch.

But just as I was leaving the foyer, a gentleman, who was standing about 25 yards away from me, threw his hand in the air and shouted enthusiastically, "Goodbye, Prophet Rob!"

I looked at him and waved back, "Bye!" Suddenly, the Spirit of the Lord came upon me in a way that I really cannot explain. A holy aggression overtook me. My friendly wave quickly turned into a commanding point, and I shouted, "Never again!" The Spirit grabbed a hold of me. I shouted again, "Never again!" I changed my direction. Instead of walking toward the stairs, I began to run toward the man. My pointed finger retracted into my fist as I neared the man. I ran all the way up to the man—this unsuspecting man who only gave me a friendly wave goodbye. I pulled back my fist, and then, using the momentum of my run, swung at him. I punched him, with as much force as I could exert, in his chest. I didn't just hit him once. I didn't just hit him twice. I hit him about four times. And then he fell to the floor.

I didn't stop there. I dove on top of the man, held him, and began to squeeze him. I shouted, "Never again! Never again! Never again will you dream of being sodomized and abused. Never again will you live in pain. Never again will you do drugs. Never again will you pick up a prostitute. Never again will you do these wicked things. I, the Lord, have come to deliver you."

I remember coming out of that prophetic frenzy, that prophetic act. I thought, *Oh, my God. What have I done?* I looked down at my hands. They were bleeding. Some of the skin on my knuckles had been ripped off. I think I cut myself on his tie pin when I was hitting him. I thought to myself, *I am going to jail. This is absolutely crazy.* I prayed, "Lord, why would You have me do such a thing?"

The Lord spoke, "Violently his life was taken away; violently I give it back unto him."

I still didn't know what to do with myself. I was standing there with blood on my suit, looking down on a man who was shaking and sobbing on the floor in the fetal position. I saw a couple of ushers standing nearby, obviously watching the entire thing. I instructed them, "Please take me to your pastor." The ushers took me to the downstairs hall, where the pastor was fellowshipping with his guests. Unsure of how to explain myself, I approached the pastor. "Pastor, may I speak with you?"

He welcomed my request, "Sure, what's going on, Prophet?"

I tried to get him aside, "We need to speak privately. Can we go somewhere and chat?"

The pastor refused, "Whatever you want to talk to me about, you can tell me openly. I have nothing to hide."

By this time, the room had become quiet and focused on me. Somewhat intimidated, somewhat embarrassed, I looked around at all of the curious pastors and church leaders. After only a moment of pause, I let it out, "Pastor, I just want to let you know that I beat up one of the guys from your church." I didn't think it was possible, but the room grew quieter.

Disrupting the silence, the pastor inquired, "Who was he?"

"Pastor, honestly, I didn't even catch his name. He was about 5 feet 9 inches, 300 pounds."

There was another pause.

"Praise the Lord!" the pastor exclaimed. "That's Phil. God used you to do what I wanted to do but couldn't—because I am his pastor. But that's exactly what he needed. Let me tell you what he did. He stole the church's tithe and offering—money that the people sowed. He used it, abused it. You see, the church recognized that he had a need. So we all put money together for him to get into an apartment. But Phil went to the apartment manager and lied. He told the manager that the church had made a mistake and needed the money back. Then Phil took that money and spent it on prostitutes and drugs. Today was his first time back to church in six weeks. It looks like God used you to do what Phil needed done in his life. But I could never do that as his pastor."

After all these years, I still see Phil from time to time. He hasn't touched drugs since that day. He hasn't picked up prostitutes either. He hasn't done any of those wicked things since his encounter with God. God completely delivered him from that moment.

Phil will usually ask me, "So, Prophet Rob, have you ever beat up anyone else like you beat me up?" I tell him that I haven't. He wears having been prophetically beaten up like a badge of honor.

Through an aggressive, prophetic act, God delivered a man from demonic influence. Truly, the prophet is called to bring exposure and elimination to demonic influence. Prophets can get to minister to even the most tightly bound souls.

THE CHALLENGE

I had just finished ministering at a large church in northern California. As I was gathering my things and preparing to leave, a gentleman approached me and made a request, "I just feel like God wants you to minister at my morning prayer meeting."

"Alright, let me pray about it." I wanted to be sure that it was the Lord. Just after I spoke those words, the Lord directed me to go. "I have sent you; you must go." I turned to the man to accept his invitation, "Actually, I don't even have to pray. God just made it clear to me that I need to be there."

The man gave me the address and the meeting time—5:00 am. That was a little early for me, but the Lord wanted me to go.

I arrived at the meeting the next day, and there were about a dozen people there to receive prophetic ministry. After the meeting, most of the people left for work. Only a few minutes after the time of ministry, everyone was gone except for a few church leaders who stayed behind to chat for a bit.

Just then, the man who had asked me to minister, who had a severe case of facial acne, approached me. (I am mentioning the acne for a reason I'll explain later in the story.) He was one of the leaders of the ministry group. Taking a condescending posture toward me, he sneered, "So, you call yourself a prophet?"

I did not like his tone, but I tried to be cordial, "No, God does."

"Well then, if you are truly a prophet of God, then tell me my life story."

He challenged me. Actually, he challenged the Holy Spirit. The spirit of prophecy moved me to prophesy with stunning accuracy and detail.

"Your story is easy," I remarked as I pointed to his wife. "You said that she ruined your life because you got her pregnant out of wedlock, and you feel like you were forced into marriage. But two years ago, you actually ruined her life when you had an affair. You had an affair because you have an unhealthy sexual appetite, and God is trying to restore your marriage." Silent, he stared at me. I continued. "As a matter of fact, God sent me here to deliver you. Nobody knows that you are unhealthy spiritually. Your sexual appetite is unsavory. There are times when your wife will deny you in the bedroom, and you become full of rage—because you are filled with demonic spirits. When your wife denies you, you leave your bedroom and approach your daughter's bedroom. Filled with unclean thoughts and set with wicked intentions, you try to go into your daughter's room. But thank God that your wife has anointed your daughter's doorway with prayer and oil. Because of your wife's prayers, the Spirit of God drives you out of your daughter's room, and you are unable to fulfill your perverse desires. After you are driven away from your daughter's room, you go downstairs. In the basement, you have a TV and a little black box that nobody knows about. Both the TV and the box are hidden within a cabinet. That black box enables you to access any channels that you want. You watch pornographic videos and pleasure yourself. Only when you finish do you feel a temporary peace come over you. Then you are able to sleep. But I have been sent here by the Lord to set you free from these demonic spirits. Do you want to be set free?"

The man's wife screamed, "Yes!" The man could barely speak, but I knew he wanted freedom. When I laid hands on him, he levitated—I mean literally levitated, floated flat on his back in the air. He shrieked, and when he shrieked, three green clouds came out of his mouth. I began to take authority over the demonic, "In the name of Jesus, I command you to be set free!" Trying to deceive me, one of the demonic beings spoke through him, "We're free!" I firmly ordered, "Even you have to go!" By that time, the man had fallen to the floor. He just remained on the floor, sobbing and shaking, as the power of God delivered him.

I prophesied over him, "As a sign to your wife that you have been fully healed and delivered, the acne that is on your face will be gone. Your skin will be renewed."

About six years later, that same man approached me at a church service where I ministered. I am happy to report that the man, who

I did not at first recognize because he seemed so different, was truly transformed. His marriage had been completely restored, and he was acne-free—a small sign of his deliverance.

The prophetic confronts the darkest parts in all of us, not to condemn us but to liberate us. So why is the prophetic so effective at expelling demonic spirits? Because the prophetic ministry is a ministry of truth, and it is the truth that liberates the human soul.

> *And you will know the truth, and the truth will set you free* (John 8:32).

As a prophet, I am called to untangle the complexities of human perversion with simple obedience to what God tells me to say. I have been given a voice that vibrates with such spiritual power that it causes demonic claws to lose their grip. Demons cower at the word of the Lord.

So whatever level of the prophetic you walk in, stir the atmosphere and let the presence of God rise up within you that you might set the captives free. Evil may present itself, but know that the power of God has already overcome.

Notes on Your Prophetic Journey

Notes on Your Prophetic Journey

CHAPTER 9

THE FUTURE REVEALED

YOU BETTER TELL GOD THEN

While fellowshipping with dear friends of mine, I felt impressed with a prophetic word for them. My friends, Jose and Angela, were not necessarily expecting the word of the Lord at that moment, but when you are linked with a prophet though covenant friendship, you are likely to receive many prophetic words—often at unexpected times, in seemingly ordinary settings.

Looking at Angela, I asked, "Angela, are you done having children?" At that moment, I already knew, by the prophetic, that they would have another child. I also knew that Angela would be shocked to hear my question. Emphatically, Angela protested, "Prophet Rob, do not get any crazy ideas!" Not even so much as acknowledging her protest, I began to prophesy, "You better tell God then, because I see a baby girl in the heavens. The Lord will use your womb one more time. He will bring forth a daughter who will bring you great joy. When she comes into the earth, she will be a blessing to your family.

The Lord says, 'She will be a prophetess to the nations, and she will be one who loves Me.'"

Within a year's time, God gave a daughter to Jose and Angela. Her name was Marisol, Mari for short.

Prophets can see a person's past. Jesus saw the past of a woman who had been married multiple times.

> *"I don't have a husband," the woman replied. Jesus said, "You're right! You don't have a husband—for you have had five husbands, and you aren't even married to the man you're living with now. You certainly spoke the truth!"* (John 4:17-18)

Prophets can see a person's current state of being. Jesus knew the thoughts of the Pharisees.

> *But when Jesus perceived their thoughts, he answering said unto them, What reason ye in your hearts?* (Luke 5:22 KJV)

And prophets can also see into the future. Jesus predicted His own crucifixion and resurrection.

> *From then on Jesus began to tell his disciples plainly that it was necessary for him to go to Jerusalem, and that he would suffer many terrible things at the hands of the elders, the*

> *leading priests, and the teachers of religious law. He would be killed, but on the third day he would be raised from the dead* (Matthew 16:21).

The future is revealed through God's prophets for various reasons. In my life and ministry, I have been graced by God to be able to see into a person's past, present, and future, whatever God chooses to show me. I feel my background as a photographer helped prepare me for ministry. A photographer has to look at three different elements in order to take a good picture—the background, subject, and the foreground. As a photographer sees the background, God will sometimes show me a person's past, filled with their hurt, pain, successes, and failures from different experiences they've gone through. The subject is the person themselves today and whatever circumstance they may find themselves in. God may also reveal the foreground, or the person's future. It could be a word of encouragement, a blessing, or a word of caution. I never know how God is going to speak or into which area of a person's life He will reveal. In the case of Angela and Jose, God was, I believe, simply announcing His blessing over them. Other times, God will use a prophet to give people directions concerning the future. That was the case with a man who was destined by God to begin a business.

TIME TO START YOUR BUSINESS

While prophesying over a friend of mine, Pastor Paul Pimentel, I prophetically discerned that God wanted him to begin his own business. At that time, Pastor Paul was working with a business partner, but I sensed that God wanted Paul to do business without a partner.

The word of the Lord came to me, "Pastor Paul, you will know that it's time to start your own company when you sit down with your business partner and he says, 'Paul, you make me so angry. You frustrate me. I feel like biting you.' When he says that he feels like biting you, that's going to be a sign to you that it is time to start your own company."

Sometime later, that very thing happened. Pastor Paul went to dinner with his business partner. During one of their conversations, Paul's business partner literally grabbed him by the hand and said, "Paul, I am so angry I could just bite you." Right then, Paul remembered the word given to him and knew it was time to begin his own company.

Over the years, Pastor Paul has become very successful in business. His company has become a multi-million-dollar corporation, and he uses his wealth to finance ministries all over the world.

God gave Paul a word about the future to help guide his path. God also reveals the future to give people hope.

PROPHESYING A PROPOSAL

About eighteen years ago in Kansas City, Kansas, I was ministering in a church. The power of God broke out in such a way that the church went into revival. There, I prophesied over a man who was nicknamed PJ. PJ was so touched by the prophetic word that I had given him that he began to invite everyone he knew to the services. Among those he invited was his former girlfriend, who was also the mother of his child.

The ex-girlfriend, along with many friends whom PJ invited, showed up to one of the services. While prophesying, the Lord gave me a word for her. As I called her forward, I asked, "PJ, who is this girl who came with your group?"

PJ seemed somewhat embarrassed, as he cringed and answered, "She's the mother of my child." He didn't even call her by name. He simply called her, "The mother of my child."

I responded, "Well, does she have a name, PJ?"

He finally gave her a proper introduction. "Yes, her name is Jen."

As I prophesied over Jen, I took the microphone and placed it behind my back. I did not want anyone to hear what I was going to tell her but her. It was a prophetic secret. "Jen, the very man you have loved your whole life—God is going to touch his heart. He's going to marry you. In three days, he's going to propose to you, and everything in your life is going to change. This is God's plan. God has heard your cry, and he's going to answer your petition."

Of course, I was prophesying to Jen about PJ. At the time, PJ was not interested in marrying Jen. In fact, he was still dating another woman. In Jen's mind, PJ proposing was an impossibility. Still, that was the word God wanted me to minister to her.

I whispered to Jen, "In three days, PJ is going to ask you to marry him. Everyone is going to ask you about what I am telling you now. They'll want to know what I am prophesying. You can tell them that it's a 'God secret.' When PJ finally proposes, however, you can tell of the word I am giving you now."

That word was given to Jen on a Wednesday night. Thursday and Friday passed with there being no sign of PJ proposing. Then came Saturday. On that Saturday, the whole church took a break from the prophetic revival so that everyone could have a chance to rest up and be refreshed before continuing the revival on Sunday.

On that Saturday, PJ randomly said to Jen, "I feel like we're supposed to hang out today. Can we go to the movies together?" Of course, Jen agreed. They met at the movies, and just before the movie began, PJ looked at Jen and said, "I don't even know why I'm doing this. But I know that I need to be a better father to our son. I know I need to be a better man. Will you marry me?"

Out of the blue, he just proposed. PJ surprised Jen. I think PJ even surprised himself.

Jen said, "Yes! And I have something to tell you. This is what the prophet whispered in my ear. He told me that in three days' time you would propose to me and that I was to say, 'yes.' This is the will of God for my life."

As I write this, Jen and PJ have been married for over eighteen years and now have three more wonderful children.

The future is full of hope, and prophets take from tomorrow's surplus and deposit it into today. As a prophet, I am called to see into the future, reach into the future, and give away the future. I love being in the prophetic ministry, because I love giving people hope. That is what the prophetic ministry does—it gives people vision for tomorrow, something to look forward to, and something to hold on to. The prophetic is meant to bring encouragement and life.

As I write to you about the hope of the future that prophets bring with them wherever they step foot, I am reminded of a certain woman.

TWINS

I was prophesying at a church in San Francisco. Attending the service was a woman who appeared exceptionally downcast. While praying for her, I found out that for several years she had been trying to become pregnant. Finally, after several years of trying, she conceived only to lose the baby in a miscarriage. She had experienced the pains of a hope deferred.

She truly was weighed down. The word of the Lord came to me for her, "Do not fear, for the Lord has heard your cry. He will not just give you one child; He will give you two. I see twin boys in your womb. One will be apostolic. One will be prophetic. And God will raise them to be powerful voices in their generation."

About a year later, I ran into the woman. She was thrilled to update me and told me that everything I prophesied had come to pass. She was indeed pregnant with twin boys.

PROPHECY AND POTENTIAL

Ultimately, what is happening when a prophet pulls from the future? He or she is tapping into the power of potential.

> *All Scripture is God-breathed and is useful for teaching, rebuking, correcting and training in righteousness, so that the servant of God may be thoroughly equipped for every good work* (2 Timothy 3:16-17 NIV).

Now watch this: "so that the servant of God may be thoroughly equipped for every good work." I love that. Do you realize that when you prophesy, you are equipping and building—or edifying—your fellow believer? That's what Paul the apostle wrote about the gift of prophecy and the other gifts of the Spirit.

> *A spiritual gift is given to each of us so we can help each other* (1 Corinthians 12:7).

The release of a prophetic word in someone's life sets things in motion. It equips the one who receives it for greater works. Prophecy pulls upon the truth of God's Word and releases a now-truth, which activates spiritual potential.

Potential is dormant or latent power. It's hidden beneath the surface, but the power of becoming what is spoken is always in the believer. Prophecy stirs that power. It agitates and causes movement. The prophetic eye sees potential, and the prophetic word digs out potential. When someone hears a prophetic word, their potential is tapped. Like waters breaking through a cracking dam, that potential begins to trickle out of dormancy and into manifestation. This is why people feel a spark or a buzzing within them as they hear a prophetic word. The prophetic is stirring things within them.

Potential is a seed, and the prophetic is water.

This is one of the many reasons why the prophetic is necessary today.

It awakens the potential that has been deposited in you—planted by the very hand of God.

There are many innovative ideas, divine assignments, and inspiring dreams hidden under the shadow of self-doubt and apathy. If all the anointed but untapped dreams and ideas hidden within the body of Christ were suddenly revealed and realized, we would have Heaven on earth. There are countless treasures uselessly buried in the soil of doubt. As a prophet, you are a spiritual treasure hunter. You seek out those hidden treasures.

Many believers have great ideas, dreams, and innovations—things they are putting off for the future. But they are stuck. They need a prophetic word to confirm how great their idea is, to stir their faith, or to quench their doubt. In many cases, because of a lack of a prophetic word, a great idea or dream remains hidden. But dreams and ideas do not want to remain hidden. Neither do hope or divine direction. They are pushing toward the surface. This is why people are drawn to prophetic people in certain seasons. There is magnetism between prophetic people and the hidden destinies within others.

Sometimes, most times, all it takes is a simple word, scripture, or encouragement to unveil destiny. That is how powerful the prophetic is. It shakes away the dust, and the hidden holy inspiration breaks for the surface and into the light of faith.

Consider the story of the prophet Elisha visiting a barren woman from Shunem. The woman, while living under the crushing emotional weight of barrenness, found the time and energy to show kindness to the man of God.

> *She said to her husband, "I am sure this man who stops in from time to time is a holy man of God. Let's build a small room for him on the roof and furnish it with a bed, a table, a chair, and a lamp. Then he will have a place to stay whenever he comes by"* (2 Kings 4:9-10).

Because the woman had given him a place to rest, the prophet Elisha offered to put in a good word for her with the king. The woman respectfully declined the prophet's gesture of gratitude. Elisha, however, was insistent; he asked his servant Gehazi, "What can we do for this woman?"

> *Gehazi replied, "She doesn't have a son, and her husband is an old man"* (2 Kings 4:14).

I imagine that Elisha was excited about the miracle that he knew was going to take place. Prophets love to deliver messages of hope. So Elisha instructed Gehazi to summon the woman. Then Elisha, Gehazi, and the woman from Shunem met together. It was then that Elisha prophesied the coming of a child. He prophesied to that which was dead within her. You see, she had the potential to bear a child. She had a womb. There was a "could have been." Perhaps the problem was with her womb, or perhaps the problem was with her husband. In fact, many theologians believe that it was the husband's age that prevented them from having children. Either way, potential was present—with only one barrier or two.

The prophet's word became like a seed—the word of God is prophetic and it is also known as seed. The prophet released a divine promise:

> *Next year at this time you will be holding a son in your arms!* (2 Kings 4:16)

And do you know what the woman said? I'll paraphrase: "No, my lord. Don't mess with your maidservant! This has been my greatest desire. Don't mess with me. I've come to accept the fact that I'm not going to have a child. I've settled it in my heart. I am going to be stuck this way."

But you see, the prophetic came to activate the truth that was in her heart. The desire of her heart was still there, though she had settled and considered it dead and gone. But the prophetic word impregnated her with hope, and that same word began to germinate and then manifested into what she was believing for. A year later, she gave birth to a son.

The prophetic word will always touch the potential within. The woman had the potential, but there was a problem. The prophetic word brought the solution. The release of the power of the prophetic will calm the chaos, silence your despair, ease your frustration, and bring the future into the now. That's exactly what it did for this couple.

JOZION

I was ministering at a church in Fresno in 2008 when I received a prophetic word from the Lord regarding the pastors. Pastors AJ and Claudia had been trying to conceive for several years, about six or seven years by this time. They were discouraged and tired of receiving prophetic words. They didn't want to *hear* any more about God having a child for them; they wanted the *fruit* of those words.

During the altar part of one of the services, I called out Pastor Claudia. I told her, "God gave you a dream about children, specifically about a son. And what I see is a son coming forth. As a matter of fact, God spoke to you in your dream that you would become pregnant, not this year but next year. And the following year you would give birth to a son." By the time I finished giving the word, she was bent over crying.

Pastor AJ, instead of rejoicing at the word of the Lord, was upset and decided to test the word. He called his wife to the front of the church and asked her in front of everyone, "Did you have a dream?"

In the midst of her sobbing, she said, "Yes, but I didn't want to tell you because I wanted God to confirm it to me." And confirm it He did, but not just with the prophetic word. The following year, Pastor Claudia had been feeling really ill. She went to the doctor, but he couldn't diagnose what was wrong. The doctor decided to do a pregnancy test. The test came back positive and confirmed the word spoken through me from the Lord. In July of 2010, Pastors AJ and Claudia had a son and named him Jozion, to whom Juanita and I are now godparents.

Notes on Your Prophetic Journey

Notes on Your Prophetic Journey

CHAPTER 10

SECRETS

EXPOSED

In the Church, there is a widespread misconception about the prophetic. Many believers are under the impression that the prophet comes to expose sin and embarrass the sinner. While there are times when sin needs to be publicly exposed, that sort of embarrassing correction is usually reserved for the stubbornly unrepentant believer. I cannot tell you how many times I have had someone shy away from me and say, "I feel like you can see all my sins." But a true prophet doesn't come to bring shame; he comes to bring grace and freedom.

I do not look to expose sin; I look to uncover the righteousness of Christ hidden within each and every believer. I am a prophet of the new covenant, not of the old. I call for the good, and I speak deliverance from the bad. The prophetic spirit wants to save, not shame.

GUN UNDER THE BED

After ministering at a church in northern California, I was invited for a fellowship at the pastor's house. After greeting some of the church members, I buckled myself in the pastor's car, and he began to drive me to his home. Just as we were pulling out of the parking lot, I noticed a brand-new orange Mustang. It turned out it belonged to the pastor's son, Paulie, who was about eighteen years old at the time.

During that period of his life, Paulie was not serving the Lord. I could see that he was in a spiritually compromised place. I could see that, like so many other pastor's kids, Paulie had become somewhat jaded, tired of going to church. I saw an opportunity to make a prophetic impact on Paulie's life.

Trying to build a bridge of relationship to Paulie, I asked him if I could go for a ride in his awesome car. With no eagerness, he allowed, "Sure."

So I jumped out of the pastor's car and into Paulie's car. "I'll see you at your house," I told the pastor. He agreed. I think he knew that I was looking to minister to his son.

So Paulie began to drive me, at high speeds, on the freeway. A car enthusiast, Paulie was quite proud of his powerful ride. We zoomed through traffic, zig-zagging around the slower vehicles. Before arriving at the house, Paulie made a stop at McDonald's, where he proceeded to do doughnuts in the restaurant parking lot. I got the full Mustang-driving experience—exhilarating.

When we arrived at the house, I followed Paulie into his room where I struck up a conversation with him. I knew that, at some point, the conversation would turn into a chance to help Paulie spiritually. I don't remember everything that was said, but I do remember that God gave me a personal insight that would shake Paulie up a bit. Knowingly, I suggested, "Let me see your gun."

Without missing a beat, Paulie defensively replied, "I don't have a gun."

"Yes, you do," I insisted.

"No, I don't," Paulie attempted to get me off the subject.

I pressed the matter even further, "As a matter of fact, I can show you exactly where it is." I stood up, walked over to Paulie's bed, and then got on my knees to look under the bed.

Paulie was busted and finally yielded, "Okay, okay, okay! I can show it to you." Paulie shot to his feet and leaned over. He went underneath the bed and revealed the shotgun that was hiding there.

Paulie had become aware of his inability to fool the prophet, so I began to name the various other things that he had hiding in his room. Remember, he was lost at that time in his life. There was a lot to hide. After I revealed what I knew about his secrets, I looked at Paulie and asked directly, "What should I do with this information that I have? Should I tell your dad?"

Without flinching, Paulie returned my glance, shrugged his shoulders, and murmured, "I don't care. Do what you gotta do."

"No. This will be our secret, and I'll be praying for you."

Because I didn't bring down the judgment that he was expecting, Paulie began to look at things just a little differently. That shift in his perspective has developed into a greater understanding of grace.

Over the years, I have become very close with Paulie and his family. Today, he is a powerful prophetic voice and a successful businessman.

Most believers would assume exposing Paulie to be the best course of action. Of course, there is a time for exposure. If someone persists in disobedience, God, in His mercy, will expose them to save them. However, exposure is God's last resort, never His first priority.

Freedom, not embarrassment, is the purpose of the prophetic word. And even when God does bring things to the forefront, He does so in a gracious way.

THE INTERPRETER

I was ministering in central California, where I saw a gentleman who was greatly distressed. Just looking at him, I could see the strain and anguish all over him. I gave him the word of the Lord, "God wants to restore your marriage. God wants to pick you up from a fall, restore your life, and restore your family. God is going to give back to you your purpose and identity."

Immediately, I turned to a lady in the church. She was sitting on the other side of the room. I began to prophesy to her. It turned out she was the wife of the man I had just finished prophesying over. They were sitting on opposite sides because things were rocky in their marriage at that point. As I ministered the word of the Lord to her, I was told that she only spoke Spanish.

"Quick. I need someone who can interpret," I announced. I pointed at another woman and asked, "You, do you speak Spanish?" She nodded. I called her forward and said, "Come here and interpret what I am saying to this woman."

So I began to prophesy to the man's wife through an interpreter. "I see that your marriage is in great distress. Your husband is being side-tracked and pulled away. But I hear the Spirit of the Lord telling me that He is removing the woman who has become a wedge between you and your husband. He's going to pull out that wedge and restore your marriage. The affair was birthed out of emotion and exists in chaos—but it will not remain. It will not live. It will end today."

The interpreter translated my every word and then added a phrase of her own. With tears in her eyes, the interpreter turned toward me, and admitted, "It's me. I am the other woman."

At that very moment, there was repentance, healing, forgiveness, and the first signs of restoration. The secret was exposed, but there was also grace.

Notes on Your Prophetic Journey

Notes on Your Prophetic Journey

CHAPTER 11

THE LITTLE THINGS

LOST KEYS

In 2002, my daughter Zoe was about a year old. I took Zoe and my wife Juanita to a furniture store. Juanita and I were looking for couches. A furniture store can be a fun place to visit as an adult, when you are imagining how nice the furniture will look in your home. But for a one-year-old, I don't think a furniture store is anything but a grueling, dull place to be. Every minute that we spent in that store crept by for our restless Zoe. She was bored.

To keep her entertained, I let her play with my keys. I do not personally find keys all that entertaining, but they did an excellent job of keeping Zoe's busy little mind occupied for the remainder of our couch hunt. Spending a considerable amount of time in the store, we walked from section to section, covered a lot of ground, and saw a lot of couches.

Finally, the time came for us to leave the store. As we approached the exit, I went to grab my keys—they weren't in my pocket. I searched myself. The keys weren't in any of my pockets. Juanita did not have them either.

That's when I remembered that Zoe had been playing with the keys. Looking at her hands, one was holding Juanita's hand, and the other hand was empty. Then, I looked back over all of the sections we had explored. I realized that my keys were somewhere in that furniture store. We had a lot of couch cushions to overturn. Actually, we had a lot of every kind of furniture to overturn.

I remember thinking, *Oh my goodness, how are we going to find the keys? That's a lot of steps to retrace.* But before we began our search, I stopped to pray. I closed my eyes, asked the Lord about my keys, and then received a vision. In my vision, I saw a vase in detail. Instead of checking randomly in compartments and seat cushions, I just looked for the vase I saw in my vision. Sure enough, I found the vase. And in the vase, I found my keys.

> *The Lord directs the steps of the godly. He delights in every detail of their lives* (Psalm 37:23).

God is interested in the little things that matter to people, so prophets should be interested in the little things that matter to people too. While many of us imagine the prophet prophesying over a nation or calling down fire from Heaven, sometimes the most significant impact the word of the Lord can make is in the mundane or everyday things. That God, the Creator of the universe, would care enough about the little troubles and concerns that we carry is astounding.

In this chapter, I want to share with you some stories that demonstrate that God cares for the "little things" in our lives.

THE STOLEN CAR

On a weeknight, at about 1:00 am, the ringing of my cell phone woke me up. When I looked at the caller ID, I saw that it was my friend, an evangelist named David Diga Hernandez. David and I are very good friends. We minister on each other's media platforms and at each other's events building the Kingdom. And, as he tells people, I often call him with the word of the Lord. In fact, sometimes when I call him, he sends my call to voicemail just in case I have a prophetic word—that way, he has the word recorded on voicemail. Again, when you have a covenant friendship with a prophet, you often get prophetic words.

So when David's call woke me up that early in the morning, we are close enough to skip the regular phone call greetings and salutations. As I answered my phone, he got right to the point, "Prophet Rob, my dad's car was stolen, and I need you to tell me where it is. Can you, please, get some prophetic insight on this matter?" At 1:00 in the morning, David *was certain* that I knew where his dad's car was located. Let's just say that he strongly believes in the prophetic gift on my life.

I live in a readied prophetic state. So, I gave him the word of the Lord, "Don't worry. I see that the car was taken by a few young men. They took it, but they aren't going to keep it, they just wanted to ride around in it. They won't take anything valuable from the car, and when the police find it, it will be located right at the border of the city of Los Angeles, under a bridge. Then the car will be returned to your dad."

When David called me later that day, he was excited, "Prophet Rob, everything you said happened. The police found my dad's car right on the outskirts of the city of Los Angeles, under a bridge, and nothing was taken. The officers are saying that someone probably just took it for a joy ride."

This is another example of how the things we might deem as a "waste of God's time" are actually quite important to Him. They are important to Him because we are important to Him.

Now I want to share a few more of these stories with you, and then I want to teach you something that I believe will forever change the way you see the prophetic.

CALL PROPHET ROB

In Victorville, California lives a really good friend of mine. I simply call him "Pastor Tommy." Pastor Tommy and I are very close. Our families are extremely close.

One day, Pastor Tommy and his daughters were all hanging out at their house. His daughters, wanting to say hello to me, said, "Dad, call Prophet Rob."

So Pastor Tommy yelled, "Prophet Rob, call me!"

The girls laughed, "Dad, you're silly. How come you didn't just call him?"

Pastor Tommy responded, "He's a prophet. He'll call me."

Within five minutes, their phone rang. It was me calling them. "Hello," Pastor Tommy greeted.

The first words out of my mouth were, "Hey, I heard you calling me. What's going on?"

Right then, his family knew that we were connected divinely. That's one of many times when I've called him in response to him simply yelling out my name.

THE KISS

While in Medellín, Colombia, a pastor friend of mine asked me to minister prophetically to a certain woman. I was ushered into the pastor's office at his church, where I was met by a mother and her daughter. I stood silent when they first walked into the room. The woman and her daughter were both speaking to each other in Spanish. I do not speak or understand Spanish, so I just waited for the pastor to enter the room and introduce us.

But while I was waiting for the pastor to enter the room, I looked at the woman as she spoke with her daughter. In the Spirit, I saw several things. I could see that the woman had been married before, and I saw that her husband had died.

Suddenly, my spirit was called outside of my body, and I found myself in the heavenly realm. In the heavens, I could see two men standing before me and a third man trying to enter the scene. From where I was, I could also see the woman and her daughter on earth—they were still casually talking. That's when I was given the knowing that the husband had been murdered by the cartel. In fact, I was given a knowing concerning many things in that woman's life. I could see so clearly in the Spirit. I thought to myself, *This is crazy.*

Just then, the pastor entered the office, and my spirit went back into my body. Immediately, I began to prophesy, "Ma'am, you are about to lose your business. You've already lost your husband, and you are in need of a certain piece of paper that shows that the business legally belongs to you. Your husband was murdered for the business. Someone is trying to steal the business from your family." By that time, the woman was weeping and affirming that what I was saying was true. I continued, "I see your husband in the heavens, and he wants you to know that he did not suffer. I also see your father. He is completely healthy. In the bottom left-hand drawer of your husband's desk there is a piece of paper in an envelope. That paper proves that the business legally belongs to you. You need to go to that desk, pull out that drawer all the way. Taped to the inside of the desk, behind that drawer, you will find the envelope with the needed document. Your husband knew his life was in danger and that others were trying to steal the company. He signed everything over to you."

Then I looked at the daughter, "And just to prove to you that this word truly is from the Lord and that your father truly is alive in Heaven, I'll tell you this. You and your father had a special kiss. Your dad would take you to school every day. When you were being dropped off, you would give your dad a kiss, get out of the car, and walk toward your school. Just when you arrived at the entrance of your school you would stop, turn around, and look back at your dad. He would then kiss two of his fingers and flip them to you. Then you would stretch out your hand, act like you caught his kiss, and place your hand on your lips. Then you would smile and walk away."

The daughter fell on the floor and began to cry, "Papá, Papá!" She told her mother, "Nobody knew about that except me and Papá."

In the end, the woman followed the voice of the Lord and searched her husband's desk. She found the document she needed in the exact place where God said it was located. The woman was able to keep her company from being taken from her because she chose to believe.

> *Believe in the Lord your God, and you shall be established; believe His prophets, and you shall prosper* (2 Chronicles 20:20 NKJV).

PRECIOUS

In Kansas City, Kansas during the year 2000, a revival broke out at a church where I was prophesying. The revival began as a three-day weekend, which then extended into several weeks, and the prophetic was intensifying as each day passed.

While I was delivering prophetic words to different people, the Lord pointed out a lady sitting in the very back of the church. "Do you see the lady in the very back? You have a word for her."

Obeying the voice of the Lord, I began to approach the woman, but God stopped me, instructing, "Not yet."

So the night went on. I prophesied over several more people, and then I again went to prophesy over the woman in the very back. Again, the Lord prevented me, "Not yet." So I continued to prophesy over even more people. All the while, the Lord held my tongue concerning the woman in the very back.

Finally, the Lord released me, "Give her the word now." But when I looked over at where the woman was sitting, she was gone. Perplexed, I inquired of the Lord, "Lord, how can I minister to her? She left."

I know the Lord's timing was intentional and perfectly orchestrated—yet sometimes we just don't understand His timing. But He will always show us His mercy. He spoke to me, "She left a little bit too early. Tell the usher, John, to get in his truck and drive down the street. On the right-hand side, about a block and a half up the road, the woman will be walking. John is to open the door and say, 'Precious young lady, you left too soon. God has a word for you.' When he tells her that, she'll get in the truck." We did as the Lord instructed, and everything happened as the Lord said it would.

When the woman walked back into the church, I was still prophesying over the people. I called out to her, "Precious, you left too soon, and God has a word for you. He heard your cry about your sister, and he's going to give you a miracle tonight. Your family is righteous. Even as Mary said, 'So be it unto me,' so has your mother said, 'So be it,' and she has placed your family, especially your brother, in My hands. Your family has been in a battle. But just as Joshua was victorious when Moses' hands were lifted up by Aaron and Hur, so your family will be victorious."

Astonished, the woman explained to me the significance of the word, "You just don't understand how powerful that word was. My name is Precious. My sister's name is Miracle. My brother's name is Joshua. And my mother's name is Mary. Our entire family has been going through it and my mom has been saying that God would take care of everything."

The entire family eventually attended that prophetic revival and received a long-awaited breakthrough.

A VISION OF GEARS

I was ministering the word of the Lord to a woman during a women's conference. While prophesying over her, I saw a peculiar vision, but being obedient to the Lord I just opened my mouth. I looked at the woman and explained, "I don't know why, but I have to say this. I see sprockets. I see a chain—like on a bicycle. I see gear shifters. The heavy gears are for when you are on flat terrain. But the big gears, the ones that are easy to pedal, are for when you are climbing hills. But you are no longer trying to go uphill, and you are no longer on flat ground. You've made it to the top. God says that it's time to shift and go downhill. It's time to learn to steer. God is leading you through the curves of your life into the finish line. You are entering a brand-new season where you are going to be blessed. The day of your struggle is over."

The woman wiped away the tears on her face and said, "That was so accurate. Two years ago, I lost my car. For the last two years, I've been riding a bike. And I felt like the Lord told me that the day of riding my bike is over. I had been complaining about it, but it wasn't until I celebrated God's provision that He made a way for me to purchase a vehicle. Now, I know that's what God wants me to do."

God has a way of speaking to exactly where you are and confirming His will—even in the little things.

Notes on Your Prophetic Journey

Notes on Your Prophetic Journey

CHAPTER 12

LAST THOUGHTS

THE SPIRIT OF PROPHECY

I want you to understand that the prophetic, in its purest form, is simple. Now, concerning the prophetic, there is much I desire to share with you. Every believer is called to live a prophetic lifestyle. You have the spirit of prophecy in you. The base scripture for the timeless truth concerning the spirit of prophecy is this:

> *Worship God, because the testimony of Jesus is the spirit of prophecy* (Revelation 19:10 CSB).

That short verse contains such a powerful revelation. The testimony of Jesus Christ Himself is the spirit of prophecy. But what does that mean? It means that all prophetic expressions—every dream, every word of knowledge, every song—emanates from the very being of Christ. He is the source of prophecy, and He is, ultimately, the message of all prophecy. The proclaiming of Him or anything reflective of His nature is the essence of prophecy.

Because the essence of prophecy is so simply Christ-centered, the prophetic turns out to abound in more of our lives than most would expect. Prophesying, for the believer, is natural and, for the most part, should be effortless. You do not even have to identify as a charismatic or a "spirit-filled believer" to prophesy. I know and love many Baptists, Methodists, and Lutherans—many of them prophesy and speak divine declarations without even realizing it.

How can this be?

Well, Jesus is the Word, and He is the spirit of prophecy. So even simply sharing what the Bible says, even quoting scripture, is a prophetic act. Furthermore, the very moment a believer, charismatic or not, shares a testimony about what Jesus has done in their life, they are prophesying. Have you ever shared about your salvation? Have you ever told of a healing you received or of a bondage that was broken off of your life? If so, then you have prophesied.

So many believers are unaware of the spirit of prophecy at work through them. Why, even a simple encouragement or uplifting word shared with a fellow believer carries the full weight of the prophetic anointing. Prophecy is a life-giving power, a simple but potent act of divine inspiration. When you speak with any divine truth and love whatsoever, you prophesy. That same inspiration gave unction to the writers of scripture.

> *For prophecy never had its origin in the human will, but prophets, though human, spoke from God as they were carried along by the Holy Spirit* (2 Peter 1:21 NIV).

Consider the time you have spent on the phone, encouraging fellow brothers and sisters in Christ through the sharing of scripture. That kind of encouragement, though often underestimated, has the power to shift a mood or lift faith. Perhaps you said, "You were on my heart, and this is what was on my heart to share with you."

What are you doing in seemingly ordinary moments like those? You are prophesying. The person on the other line might not know; you might not even know. But if you are encouraging them with truth—truth that is grounded in the Word—then you are giving them a testimony of Christ, and that is prophecy. When you, by faith, gaze into the future to see and declare a brighter day, you are prophesying. Look again at our key verse.

> *Worship God, because the testimony of Jesus is the spirit of prophecy* (Revelation 19:10 CSB).

In that verse, the word *testimony* captures my attention. When you understand the power of your testimony, you can understand the power of the spirit of prophecy.

YOUR TESTIMONY

The word *testimony* in Greek is *maturia*. The word *maturia* simply means this: evidence given. Whether it is revealing the future or a word of knowledge that reveals secrets, past or present, prophecy is evidence. It is evidence that is given to a believer or a non-believer. Prophecy is a record. It is something that is stated and remembered; it serves as a spiritual marker. It is also a report or a witness account.

As a prophetic vessel, you are a witness to whatever is being revealed. As a prophet, you are a witness of the future, reporting on what you see. You are a witness of people's past hurts and present circumstances—and you supernaturally report on these matters. You give a testimony about what God shows you.

Think back to the example I gave earlier. Let's say you call a friend on the phone. They are discouraged, but you give them an encouraging word about their future. You, by faith, are looking at what will be and giving a testimony of that account. Even though you do not necessarily see details, you know that the goodness of God will lead them to peace. Just the knowing and declaring of that truth is prophecy. You may not see it in that way, but I want to challenge your paradigm. Testimony means "given evidence" and it also means witnessing for Christ. What evidence is given in that situation? It's your faith; that's the evidence.

> *Now faith is the substance of things hoped for, the evidence of things not seen* (Hebrews 11:1 KJV).

That testimony is not just backed by your faith; it is backed by the Word. And so when you begin to prophesy, you also begin to share God's Word—by book, chapter, or verse. In fact, when you testify of the Word, you are moving in the fundamental realm of the spirit of prophecy—the revealing of the Lord Jesus Christ through the Word. If I were to ask most believers, "Have you ever prophesied over someone?" they would answer in the negative. But if I were to ask the same group, "Have you ever shared a Bible verse with someone?" they would likely answer in the affirmative. Have you ever given somebody a verse? Again, that is prophecy. How? You are testifying about the truth and ultimately about Christ; once again, that is prophecy.

We need both the Word, which is the source of our testimony, and worship, which is the source of our intimacy. The two flow hand in hand.

THE PROPHETIC SPIRIT

Though not everyone is called to the office of the prophet, as I am, everyone can flow in the prophetic spirit in one form or another. Remember, it could be in the midst of sharing a cup of coffee with a group of friends, and you start sharing about Christ. It might be talking about last Sunday's sermon to a co-worker or a devotional that really ministered to you during the week.

Suddenly your spirit-man begins to leap at what is being shared and you find hope or encouragement, but you also bring hope and encouragement to another. This is how the spirit of prophecy works and how everyone can flow in it. It is encouragement by words, fellowship, scriptures, texts, or someone testifying about the miracle-working power of God.

> *But one who prophesies strengthens others, encourages them, and comforts them* (1 Corinthians 14:3).

When you prophesy, it should cause something to happen within the one who is receiving the prophetic word, whether it be feeling comforted or built up in their spirit. This is because God's Spirit is contagious. His word has a frequency; it has a sound that can break through any wall of opposition.

In order to break through any obstacle or limitation, something stronger is needed. This is why, as we minister prophetically, it is always done in love.

> *Love never fails* (1 Corinthians 13:8 NKJV).

And because God is love, He will never fail. You can be assured as you walk through this prophetic life, God will always be there with you. He is always longing to speak to you. Take the time to listen.

- Know that you are a child of God and He wants to pour His best into you.
- Consecrate yourself by setting aside time to be with the Lord.

- Obey the leading of His voice.
- Have faith and believe in what God can do in you and through you.
- Find yourself worshiping in His presence.
- Submit yourself and become accountable to your church and the leadership where God has placed you.
- And in everything, as you strengthen, encourage, and comfort others, do it all in love.

There is much more I could say about the prophetic, but that will have to be for another book. God has done so much in my life, and I have been blessed to have the opportunity not only to minister the word of God but also to minister to His people. I hope that by reading this book, it has not only encouraged you but also given you insight into the mighty miracles God can do through you when you yield yourself to His voice.

Allow the spirit of prophecy to awaken within you!

Notes on Your Prophetic Journey

Notes on Your Prophetic Journey

ABOUT ROB SANCHEZ

Prophet Rob Sanchez, called by God to the Body of Christ, encourages every generation he encounters to awaken to God's Kingdom within them. Through a timely message from the Spirit of God, believers have been released into their God-given destinies and flourish within their local church. He and his wife, Juanita, are also busy with the joy of raising three daughters in central California.

Join today!
lovetoreadclub.com

Inspiring Articles
Powerful Video Teaching
Resources for Revival

Get all of this and so much more, e-mailed to you twice weekly!